T0054371

FIVE-MINUTE
DEVOTIONS
FOR
MEN

HARVEST HOUSE PUBLISHERS
EUGENE, OREGON

MILANO SOFTONE is a trademark of The Hawkins Children's LLC. Harvest House Publishers, Inc. is the exclusive licensee of the trademark MILANO SOFTONE.

Cover by Studio Gearbox
Cover image © Alex Landa, Ton Photographer 4289 / Shutterstock
Interior design by Matt Shoemaker Design

For bulk, special sales, or ministry purchases, please call 1-800-547-8979.
Email: CustomerService@hhpbooks.com

This logo is a federally registered trademark of the Hawkins Children's LLC. Harvest House Publishers, Inc., is the exclusive licensee of this trademark.

The content in this book is excerpted and updated from *Five-Minute Bible Workouts for Men*, *Five-Minute Faith Builders for Men*, and *Five Minutes in the Bible for Men*.

Five-Minute Devotions for Men (Milano Softone™)
Copyright © 1998, 2006, and 2010 by Bob Barns
Published by Harvest House Publishers
Eugene, Oregon 97408
www.harvesthousepublishers.com

ISBN 978-0-7369-8988-6 (Milano Softone™)
ISBN 978-0-7369-8989-3 (eBook)

Library of Congress Control Number: 2023947026

Printed in China

24 25 26 27 28 29 30 31 32 / RDS / 10 9 8 7 6 5 4 3 2 1

To you—the man reading this book

Statistics tell us men don't read. Therefore,
because you break the stats, you're to be complimented.
You're a reader!

And even more than a reader, you're a man who wants to
become more like Jesus. This can happen in many ways,
but I've found that one is a willingness to read,
apply, and grow.

So my prayer is that, as you read these devotions,
the Spirit of God will build you into a better man—
and if you're married, a better husband, and if you're a dad, a
better father—and more conformed to
the image of Jesus Christ.

May these daily nuggets enrich your life.

Be Thankful and Content in All Things

Bless the Lord, O my soul; and all that is within me,
bless His holy name. Bless the Lord, O my soul,
and forget none of His benefits.

Psalm 103:1-2

Two of the greatest words in the English language are *Thank you*. That's why when their children are still very young, parents begin teaching them to say "Thank you." When someone gives them a gift or a compliment—and before they can even utter the words—they jump right in with, "Now, what do you say?"

But as we grow from childhood to adulthood, we often forget our manners and hold back from expressing our appreciation to someone who does us a service.

It's the same way with God. He loves to hear that we're thankful for all He bestows on us. He is the provider of all we have. In Ecclesiastes 2:24–25, we read, "There is nothing better for a man than to eat and drink and tell himself that his labor is good. This also I have seen, that it is from the hand of God. For who can eat and who can have enjoyment without Him?"

Thankful hearts give thanks. As I've grown older, I've looked back over this short life and realized that God has been faithful all along the way. He's always provided for all our needs. Not necessarily for our wants, but always for our needs. That's totally in keeping with the words of 2 Peter 1:3: "His divine power has granted to us everything pertaining to life and godliness, through the true knowledge of Him who called us by His own glory and excellence."

The password for entering into God's presence is two words: "Thank You." In his writings, Paul told us to be content in all situations (Philippians 4:11). When we're restless and find ourselves discontented with our lives and situations, it's accentuated when we don't have a heart that readily gives thanks. First Thessalonians 5:18 says, "In everything give thanks; for this is God's will for you in Christ Jesus."

Let's not take anything for granted. Let's be thankful and content in all things.

Today's Action
Evaluate the thankfulness of your heart. How can it be improved?

Prayer
Father God, don't let me forget to always be thankful
for what You do for me. You are a gracious God
who continually pours out blessings on my life.
Thank You for everything—big and small. Amen.

GODLY HONOR

Jesus said to them, "You do not know what you are asking.
Are you able to drink the cup that I drink?"

MARK 10:38

Many times we ask God for things without realizing the price to be paid if we receive them. James and John asked Jesus if they could sit at His right and left, not realizing the cost of that request. They wanted the honor of sitting close to him, but they had no idea a cross had to be borne along with that honor.

We pray to God and ask to be the best husband, the best worker, the best baseball player, the best salesperson, or the best father without taking time to figure out what cost our request will make on our lives. Great requests or supplications with shallow motives can turn out to be overwhelming when God answers them. And great requests or supplications with stately motives for God's grace may often be granted, but not in the way we might expect.

Godly honor is not lightly won. We must be ready to pay the price in time, trials, sacrifice, love, or money.

Today's Action

Before you ask God for something, make sure you realize what the cost might be.

Prayer

Father God, thank You for making me aware of the cost of serving others. Help me take time today to count the cost of being one of Your disciples—and then give You praise for allowing me to serve You. Amen.

Always or Usually?

[Love] always protects, always trusts,
always hopes, always perseveres.
1 Corinthians 13:7 niv

It's hard for us mere mortals to adequately understand the word *always*. In today's culture, we don't completely realize what this kind of commitment means. When we say always, don't we usually mean sometimes...or most of the time? But always really means eternal and everlasting. Knowing this, can anyone commit to always?

When Scripture says always, it means always—never changing, dependable until death. And so I'm challenged by what Paul says love always does:

- It protects.
- It trusts.
- It hopes.
- It perseveres.

I so want my life to be defined by that kind of love. I want to be a man who's known for his word. And I often advise others, "Just do what you say you're going to do." As we grow older and look back over life's journey, may we know that love and what it encompasses is indeed the true victory of life.

Today's Action

Tell your family that, with God's help, you'll always love them.

Prayer

Father God, give me the strength and perseverance to—without hesitation—truthfully say I'll always love my family. Amen.

We Are the Prodigals

*While he was still a long way off, his father saw him
and was filled with compassion for him; he ran to his son,
threw his arms around him and kissed him.*

This part of the prodigal son parable is one of the most moving scenes in the whole Bible. I can picture the father, with his accelerated heartbeat, seeing his wayward son approaching home after he'd squandered his inheritance money and was forced to slop pigs to survive.

This story reflects our heavenly Father, who runs to us when we're desperate, at our rope's end after experiencing the pitfalls of life and in pursuit of the true meaning of life. In our search, we may not have reached rock bottom like this son did, but all of us have tried to find purpose in making our own way.

The prodigal tells his father he's not worthy to be taken back as a son, but that doesn't prevent the father from loving him, forgiving him, and bringing out the very best upon his return. This is the way our heavenly Father treats us and welcomes us back—with open arms.

Today's Action

Forgive someone for something you've considered unforgivable.

Prayer

Father God, thank You for forgiving me while
I was walking in sin. Amen.

RULES FOR LIVING

Love the Lord your God with all your heart
and with all your soul and with all your mind
and with all your strength.

MARK 12:30 NIV

We are a culture of independence:

"Let me do my own thing."

"I know what's best for me."

"Don't tell me what to do."

But Mark 12:30, a rule for life, gives us the boundaries in which to live. J. Wilbur Chapman stated, "Anything that dims my vision of Christ or takes away my taste for Bible study or cramps my prayer life or makes Christian work difficult is wrong for me, and I must, as a Christian, turn away from it."[1]

Review your lifestyle to evaluate how you're doing with your choices of late. Are they drawing you closer to our Lord or sending you farther away from Him? Do you still have the same hunger for God's Word you used to? Do you still have quiet times with Him? Are your prayers as fervent as before? Do you still enjoy spending time with other believers?

If the answer to any of those questions is no, guess who's moved away. Follow God's rule for living, and remain close to Him.

Today's Action

Evaluate your choices to determine if they glorify the Lord Jesus Christ.

Prayer

Father God, help me be honest in my self-appraisal,
and may my choices honor You. Amen.

Released from Darkness

He has sent me to bind up the brokenhearted, to proclaim freedom
for the captives and release from darkness for the prisoners.
Isaiah 61:1 niv

The good news of Christ is freedom. We who are captives to the hard things of life can be set free—no longer bound by our own prisons. Our Scripture today—and through verse 3 of Isaiah 61—gives many examples of God's provision:

- He binds up the brokenhearted.
- He proclaims freedom for the captives.
- He releases prisoners from the darkness.
- He comforts all who mourn.
- He bestows a crown of beauty instead of ashes.
- He gives the oil of gladness instead of mourning.
- He gives a garment of praise instead of a spirit of despair.
- He calls us oaks of righteousness, a planting of the Lord.

Why? For the "display of His splendor" (verse 3 niv). We no longer need to look at the dark side of life. William R. Alger said, "After every storm the sun will smile; for every problem there is a solution, and the soul's indefensible duty is to be of good cheer."[2] Our glass can be half full when others see it as half empty. When we rely on God, we're released from the darkness and into the light.

Today's Action

Take a negative and turn it into a positive.

Prayer

Father God, may others see me as an oak of righteousness, and let all that happens to me be a display of Your splendor. Amen.

The Secret to Abundance

Whoever sows generously will also reap generously...
for God loves a cheerful giver.
2 Corinthians 9:6-7 niv

Not only is 2 Corinthians 9:6-7 a godly principle for life, but it's applicable to the believer as well as to the unbeliever. Some of my most generous friends are nonbelievers, yet they've somehow caught the secret to abundance in life.

As Christians, however, we have an extra blessing in that God loves a cheerful giver. Martin Luther said, "I have held many things in my hands, and I have lost them all; but whatever I have placed in God's hands, that I still possess."[3]

We had a saying around our home: "You can't out-give God." This is so true. Whenever we give, we seem to abundantly reap God's riches. As a young man, I didn't trust others with my money, time, talent, or possessions until one day I realized it was all God's in the first place. When I started to trust Him with all of these things, I found out He took better care of them than I did—and He blessed me abundantly.

Today's Action

Give something away with no expectation of anything in return.

Prayer

Father God, help me learn to give generously to those who are in need. I want to be known as a cheerful giver. Amen.

REFRESHED BY GOD

[Elijah] prayed that he might die...Then he lay down under the bush
and fell asleep. All at once an angel touched him and said,
"Get up and eat." He looked around, and there by his head
was some bread baked over hot coals, and a jar of water.
1 KINGS 19:4-6 NIV

Sometimes we ask ourselves, *Is God really interested in my physical welfare? Does He care if I eat or sleep?* Yes, God does care for our personal needs on a daily basis. Much of the four Gospels deals with eating and sleeping. In many situations of everyday life, Jesus had the same basic needs we do. After a hard day's work or journey, He was hungry, thirsty, and sleepy. We serve a God who, through Jesus, experienced the same daily requirements we have.

We must learn to trust Jesus with all of our needs. We don't have to doubt or wonder if He takes care of us, even in the little things in life. Clearly, Scripture shows us that He cares for us and will provide for the smallest of our needs.

What are some of your smallest needs? Trust God to provide for those concerns and refresh you whenever you're weary.

Today's Action

Consider how God has both provided for and refreshed you in the past.

Prayer

Father God, thank You for being interested in my needs. I appreciate Your concern, and I know You'll both provide what I need and bring me refreshment. Amen.

Strong, Gentle Hands

He showed them his hands.

Luke 24:40 niv

Do you take your hands for granted? Are your fingers and thumbs just ten appendages that happen to be there? Sometimes we don't really appreciate what God has given us. We do so much with our hands, but even the slightest injury makes us aware of the importance of a finger, a thumb, or our palm. We can't lift, tie, open, squeeze, or perform many other tasks if we can't manipulate our hands as God created them to be used.

While Jesus walked this earth, His hands were, of course, human. And because of His carpentry trade and journeying in the hot, Mediterranean climate of the Middle East, they were most likely strong and rough. Yet they blessed little children, and they touched the sick and made them well in mind, spirit, and body. In John 10:28, Jesus Himself gives us an image of His saving hands, both then and now: "I give them eternal life, and they shall never perish; no one can snatch them out of my hands" (niv).

On the cross, the wounded hands of Jesus paid the price for our sins. As we look at our hands today, may we remember the price Jesus paid with His.

Today's Action

Look at your hands and thank God for creating them to do so many things.

Prayer

Father God, I thank You for my hands.
May I use them to Your glory. Amen.

But as for Me…

If serving the Lord seems undesirable to you,
then choose for yourselves this day whom you will serve,
whether the gods your ancestors served beyond the Euphrates,
or the gods of the Amorites, in whose land you are living. But
as for me and my household, we will serve the Lord.

Joshua 24:15 niv

Joshua was a wise man who knew that in his latter days of life, his countrymen would end up following some type of god. And so he made a strong public declaration that he and his family were going to serve the Lord.

We dads need to be so bold with our families. Is your family waiting patiently for you to step forward and make the same declaration? Are they waiting for you to join them in following Jesus? The Scripture is clear—as a husband and father, you are to serve the Lord and model that service in your household.

Men, step forward and proclaim this to all those with listening ears: that you're taking the initiative and declaring which God you and your family will serve.

Today's Action
Declare that you and your household will serve the Lord.

Prayer
Father God, please give me a brave heart in making the proclamation to serve You. Amen.

Raising Healthy Children

*By wisdom a house is built, and through understanding
it is established; through knowledge its rooms
are filled with rare and beautiful treasures.*

Proverbs 24:3-4 NIV

So many couples have asked my wife, Emilie, and me how to raise a healthy family, and we tell them we always came back to the three basic principles of this passage in Proverbs. We raised our family with:

- wisdom
- understanding
- knowledge

If we as parents all do this, our rooms will be filled with rare and beautiful treasures—children who are obedient, polite, and considerate, and who honor God.

When we're out in public and observe a healthy, functioning family, we know they've been directly or indirectly observing these three important guidelines. How do we know? Because we can see the rewards—or blessings—of that training. The parents have rare and beautiful treasures.

Is it easy to be so blessed? No. It takes a lot of work and stick-to-it discipline to have these treasures. But when your goal is to raise healthy children, you have to believe in the results.

Today's Action

Declare that you're going to raise your children with wisdom, understanding, and knowledge.

Prayer

Father God, I want the rooms of my home to be filled with rare and beautiful treasures. Thank You for Your help as I work to make it so. Amen.

Impressed on Our Hearts

Love the LORD your God with all your heart and with all your soul
and with all your strength...Impress [these] on your children.
Talk about them when you sit at home and when you walk
along the road, when you lie down and when you get up.
DEUTERONOMY 6:5, 7 NIV

Deuteronomy 6:5-7 encourages us to love the Lord our God with all our hearts and with all our souls and with all our strength. We're impressed, then, to have this commandment on our hearts and to teach it to our children when we're talking with them at home, when we're taking a walk with them along the road, when we're all going to bed, and when we're getting up. Wow, it sounds like we need to be ready to make spiritual applications at all times!

Anytime and anywhere we can teach godly principles, we should. Use every event to talk about the good and the bad of life. Help your children develop their own theological grids for life so they can make independent conclusions about what's right and what's wrong based on the Bible.

Impress God's Word on your heart—and then share it with not just your children but with everyone in your life.

Today's Action

If you're a dad with children still at home, find a current event that has spiritual implications. Then teach your children how to reach a sound, God-pleasing conclusion about what's right and what's wrong regarding that issue.

Prayer

*Father God, help me apply Your spiritual truths
to all of the events in my life. Amen.*

Making Godly Decisions

Seek first his kingdom and his righteousness,
and all these things will be given to you as well.
MATTHEW 6:33 NIV

In the Sermon on the Mount (Matthew 5–7), Jesus addresses questions regarding concerns about earthly needs such as clothing, food, and what to drink. He explains that pagans run after all these things, but believers should depend on the heavenly Father for them: "Do not worry about tomorrow, for tomorrow will worry about itself. Each day has enough trouble of its own" (Matthew 6:34 NIV).

This verse out of the book of Matthew was our family's theme verse. When in doubt about an important life decision, we would ask ourselves, "Are we attempting to seek first the kingdom of God, or are we running after our own desires?" It's amazing how clear the answer could be when we asked this basic question. And within a day or two, it would be quite apparent that we'd made the right decision.

We've found that both children and parents love having a "family" verse, and Matthew 6:33 is a perfect verse for making godly decisions.

Today's Action

Choose a theme verse for your family. (Remember, it can always be changed at a later date.)

Prayer

Father God, thank You for giving us inspired Scripture that helps us make good decisions in life. Amen.

MADE FOR THE LORD

He himself is our peace.
EPHESIANS 2:14 NIV

I've always loved the peaceful feeling of coming home. After a hectic day of work, driving on the freeway, and hearing the loud noises of the world, my heart would long for the comforts of home.

I also realized that peace doesn't just happen in one's life. But many of my friends were looking in all the wrong places, trying to find it through jobs, material possessions, vacations, clothes, or entertainment. They eventually learned that peace wasn't found in these things. Only when they realized they were made for the Lord did they find tranquility. Saint Augustine said, "Lord, Thou madest us for Thyself, and we can find no rest till we find rest in Thee!"[4] There will be no rest or peace for us until we get it from Jesus.

People often ask, "What is the purpose of life?" Ephesians 2:14 and the quote from Saint Augustine give us an idea of the answer. It's to find peace with our Lord. The peacefulness of our home—and our life—is based on the fact that we were made by our Lord Jesus Christ and have come to know Him.

Today's Action

If you aren't sure you know Jesus as your Lord and Savior, search out a friend who can share what it means to know Jesus or contact a local, Bible-based church and talk to someone there. If you are sure, consider whether you're prepared to share the way to salvation when asked.

Prayer

Father God, thank You for giving me Your peace, and help me always find my peace in You. Amen.

The More We Listen

When there are many words, transgression is unavoidable,
but he who restrains his lips is wise.

Proverbs 10:19

Eleanor Roosevelt once stated:

> A mature person is one who does not think only in absolutes, who is able to be objective even when deeply stirred emotionally, who has learned that there is both good and bad in all people and in all things, and who walks humbly and deals charitably with the circumstances of life, knowing that in this world no one is all knowing and therefore all of us need both love and charity.[5]

Proverbs 10:19 suggests that we be more of a listener than a talker. After all, the habit of speaking too many words can lead to putting our foot in our mouth. The more we speak, the greater the chance of our saying something offensive. But the wise person will restrain their speech. God gave us one tongue and two ears, so I suppose He wanted us to listen twice as much as we speak.

Listening seldom gets us into trouble, but our mouths can certainly cause transgressions. The more we listen, the more we'll learn.

Today's Action

In any conversation you have today, concentrate on listening at least twice as much as you speak.

Prayer

Father God, thank You for giving me two good ears to hear, and help me be a better listener. Amen.

SINGING HIS SONG

Behold, God is my salvation, I will trust and not be afraid;
for the LORD GOD is my strength and song.
ISAIAH 12:2

Billy Graham once stated, "Being a Christian is more than just an instantaneous conversion—it is a daily process whereby you grow to be more and more like Christ."[6] Many men want to accept God like they would accept a fire insurance policy, but they aren't willing to make Him their Lord.

When Jesus becomes our salvation, we receive His courage, strength, and song. It doesn't all happen overnight, though. To become more and more like Christ is a lifelong process.

The 1928 *Book of Common Prayer* includes this appeal to believers:

> Go forth into the world in peace. Be of good courage. Hold fast that which is good. Render to no one evil for evil. Strengthen the fainthearted. Support the weak. Help the afflicted. Show love to everyone. Love and serve the Lord, rejoicing in the power of the Holy Spirit; and the blessing of almighty God, the Father, the Son, and the Holy Spirit, be among you and remains with you always.[7]

Let Jesus become your salvation, and sing His song all of your days.

Today's Action

Take at least one step to grow to be more like Jesus, trusting Him for your courage, strength, and song.

Prayer

Father God, I don't want to be just a Sunday Christian. Please give me a new song each day, and thank You for Your strength. Amen.

Overcoming Discouragement

Where can we go? Our brothers have made us lose heart.
They say, "The people are stronger and taller than we are;
the cities are large, with walls up to the sky."
Deuteronomy 1:28 niv

How often have you been told you aren't good enough? You're too short, your hair is too thin, your lips are too small, your voice is too soft, you can't carry a tune, or your nose has a bump on it. There's nothing new about hearing words of discouragement. Even in Moses' time, people were told negative things about themselves.

What a misfortune that friends, teachers, and parents sometimes put stumbling blocks in our way by discouraging us with words of fear, guilt, hate, and inferiority. We must not heed those who would destroy our dreams by saying unkind words or criticizing us—and trying to make us lose confidence and stumble.

God sent Jesus to us, His children, so we would be delivered from these evils. In Him, we can have the courage to overcome what we experience from the negative people in our lives. We're able to rise above insults and discouraging words, focusing instead on what God has given us. Winston Churchill once stated, "Courage is rightly esteemed the first of human qualities...because it is the quality which guarantees all the others."[8] When we have the courage that comes from God, we can overcome discouragement.

Today's Action

Let God give you the courage to overcome the effects of encountering a negative person or situation today.

Prayer

Father God, thank You for giving me courage to overcome the negativity of the world. Amen.

THE GIFT

All things come from You,
and from Your hand we have given You.
1 CHRONICLES 29:14

Imagine what a heavy schedule of appointments President Abraham Lincoln had day after day. But still, he agreed to see an elderly woman who simply asked to see him:

> As she entered Lincoln's office, he rose to greet her and asked how he might be of service. She replied that she had not come to ask a favor. She had heard that the President liked a certain kind of cookie, so she had baked some for him and brought them to his office. With tears in his eyes, Lincoln responded, "You are the very first person who has ever come into my office asking not, expecting not, but rather bringing me a gift. I thank you from the bottom of my heart."[9]

I get so excited when others come to me with a gift rather than a request. How much more must God rejoice when we don't bring Him a list of requests but instead simply give Him the gift of our gratitude and love. Nothing pleases our heavenly Father more than our sincere thanksgiving.

Today in your prayer time, concentrate on the sacrifice of praise, giving thanks for the gift of God's mercy and holiness.

Today's Action

Give the gift of praise to our heavenly Father, who is the giver of all good gifts.

Prayer

Father God, I want to let You know I'm thankful for all You do for me. And thank You for Your mercy and holiness. Amen.

The Sky's the Limit

Grow in the grace and knowledge
of our Lord and Savior Jesus Christ.
2 Peter 3:18 niv

Even though I played a lot of basketball in high school and college, I'm awed watching today's players. In my day, a six-foot guard, a six-foot forward, and a six-five center were about what you would expect in a starting lineup. Today, many six-eight guards dribble with the ease and finesse of a much shorter player of old.

To predict how tall we might become, we must depend on our inherited genetic factors. Regardless of what we do, we stop growing at a certain height. Our stature is predetermined.

Our potential for spiritual growth, however, knows no such bounds. The sky's the limit. We can grow as spiritually tall as we want. But in order to grow spiritually, we must exercise our faith regularly—talking to the Lord, reading His Word, and obeying His teachings. When we draw close to God, He will produce the likeness of Christ in us.

Today's Action

Deliberately step out in faith in some way, trusting in the Lord to help and guide you.

Prayer

Father God, take my heart and my hands and help me grow. I want to be a spiritual giant. Amen.

ETERNAL DIVIDENDS

Beware, and be on your guard against every form
of greed; for not even when one has an abundance
does his life consist of his possessions.

LUKE 12:15

Have you ever heard the saying, "He who dies with the most toys wins"? I think some men actually believe this is true! I'm not saying we shouldn't have a nice car or home, a boat, an ATV, a set of water skis, or other possessions. But if these are all we work and strive for, in time we'll be disappointed. Possessions by themselves will not give meaning to life.

In Luke 12:16-21, Jesus tells a parable about a man who spent his life gathering more and more wealth but had no time for God. This individual was a man of great wealth, but he became bankrupt in death.

We need to invest our lives in activities that pay eternal dividends. One of the great financial principles of this world is called "compound interest." Compound interest charts show overwhelming growth of our principle funds when we continue to invest in our account and reinvest the interest.

That same principle also works in the life of the believer. If we invest in eternal things of value, the Lord will bless us with abundance. A life lived for Christ has eternal dividends.

Today's Action

Ponder this question: "Where is your treasure?"

Prayer

Father God, please make me sensitive to the value of possessions.
When I want one more toy, remind me to ask myself if it will be
of eternal value. Amen.

"I Quit!"

Let us not lose heart in doing good,
for in due time we shall reap if we do not grow weary.

Galatians 6:9

As we look at people in our jobs, churches, neighborhoods, and at social gatherings, we sometimes observe individuals who seem to have it all. And in many cases, nonbelievers seem to be getting all the breaks in life. We try to do all the right things, but life just isn't working. At times we want to shout, "What's the use? I quit!"

Perseverance and endurance are character qualities that often aren't a lot of fun to acquire. In order to get them, we have to be long in suffering—and that's hard.

If you feel like you're facing hopeless circumstances in your life, don't give up. God promises that if we stick with it, if we plant good seeds and good deeds, we'll obtain good results in time. Keep going. Have faith and keep up your good works. Do your best, especially for those in need. Be not weary in serving.

Today's Action

Resolve to do a good deed for someone who seems to have no hope.

Prayer

Father God, rekindle my faith. Help me do my best when I assist others. Amen.

Heaven on Earth?

This is my comfort in my affliction,
that Your word has revived me.

Psalm 119:50

Many religious teachers try to alter what the Bible teaches. They say once you become a Christian, living the rest of your life will be similar to how you'll live in heaven. They say you'll somehow become wealthy, healthy, and wise—and that nothing bad will ever happen to you. But this is not what the Bible teaches. All throughout history, God-fearing believers have been caught in circumstances so terrible that the results are nearly indescribable, such as in war and with famine and torture. Even death.

In Hebrews 11:35-38, we're told that believers often suffer, and I've found that's true. God doesn't always lift us out of difficult circumstances. Usually, He comes into our situation and meets us where we are. Jesus becomes the light within our darkness.

God never promised a life of earthly perfection, but He did promise to always stand beside us and never forsake us (Deuteronomy 31:6; Hebrews 13:5). And He'll give us strength and the grace to rejoice even when we're in trying—even terrible—situations, coming down from heaven to meet us here on earth.

Today's Action

Are you experiencing a darkness now? Ask Jesus to bring His light into it.

Prayer

Father God, thank You that I don't have to fear the darkness that sometimes surrounds me. I know You are with me and will give me real peace despite my circumstances. Amen.

The Foundation for Marriage

What therefore God has joined together,
let no man separate.

Mark 10:9

When I was growing up, it was unheard of for Christian couples to divorce. But unfortunately, today Christian marriages seem to be ending in divorce equal to those in the secular population. What's gone wrong? Where have we lost our focus and commitment in marriage?

Dietrich Bonhoeffer, the great German pastor who was killed in a World War II Nazi prison camp, wrote a book titled *Letters and Papers from Prison*. In this reflection of life, he wrote a wedding sermon and made several points that should be stressed in our day of "chipped" marriages. In my own words, they included:

- God is guiding.
- God makes the union indissoluble.
- God places on marriage both blessing (children) and burden (caring and providing for the family).
- Christ is the foundation of a marriage.[10]

According to both Bonhoeffer's sermon and God's Word, these are the building blocks for a successful marriage. If you're married, remember them when the foundation of your marriage feels shaky.

Today's Action

Looking at Bonhoeffer's four points, assess how you're doing in your marriage individually and as a couple. Then work to strengthen your weak areas.

Prayer

Father God, may I be sensitive to those areas of my life and my marriage that need more effort from me. Amen.

An Attitude of Prayer

Be anxious for nothing, but in everything
by prayer and supplication with thanksgiving
let your requests be made known to God.
Philippians 4:6

What is the proper posture in prayer? As I've grown in my Christian walk, I've pondered that basic question. I sincerely want to be pleasing to God in my posture of prayer.

In searching Scripture, I realized that great liberty is given to praying people. The important point is that our hearts are in communication with God. And in the Scriptures, we discover many "attitudes" of prayer:

- kneeling (1 Kings 8:54; Ezra 9:5; Daniel 6:10; Acts 20:36)
- standing (Jeremiah 18:20)
- sitting (2 Samuel 7:18)
- lying prostrate (Ezekiel 11:13)
- in bed (Psalm 63:6)
- in private (Matthew 6:6; Mark 1:35)
- with others (Psalm 35:18)
- anywhere (1 Timothy 2:8)
- silently (1 Samuel 1:13)
- loudly (Acts 16:25)
- for everything (Genesis 24:12-14; Philippians 4:6; 1 Timothy 2:1-2)
- at all times (Luke 18:1)

Prayer is more than your posture. The most important part of prayer is your attitude and your heart.

Today's Action

Beginning today and throughout the week, try several of the different physical positions listed here as you pray. Read the Scripture that goes with each, and notice how you feel in each posture.

Prayer

Father God, help me remember that You're not as concerned with my posture as You are with my daily communication with You. Amen.

The Power of Gentleness

We proved to be gentle among you,
as a nursing mother tenderly cares
for her own children.

1 Thessalonians 2:7

One of the great compliments we can receive is that of being gentle. We don't often think of gentleness as a masculine trait, but Paul, Silvanus, and Timothy were compassionate, spiritual mentors to the Thessalonian church. They were rugged men who were, according to Scripture, gentle. They also exhorted, comforted, and admonished the Thessalonians as a father does with his children (1 Thessalonians 2:11).

While raising my children, I considered myself a strict father. My daughter, however, recently commented that she considered me a very gentle dad. That was a pleasant surprise to me. We need gentleness when we teach our children how to reflect God's glory. Then we can rejoice when we see where they are spiritually in their lives and where their children are in theirs.

Barnes' Notes on the Bible says, "Ministers of the gospel should be gentle, tender, and affectionate...What is wrong we should indeed oppose—but it should be in the kindest manner toward those who do wrong."[11] Remember, there is power in gentleness.

Today's Action

Apply gentleness toward others today and discover the power of gentleness.

Prayer

*Father God, may others see me as You are—
both strong and gentle. Amen.*

A "Breaking Up" Process

Consider it all joy...when you encounter various trials,
knowing that the testing of your faith produces endurance.
James 1:2-3

Many times we attempt to acquire a godly trait without first properly preparing the soil of our lives. Growing up on a farm, I learned how difficult it is to prepare the soil before planting. We had a lot of rocks, and we had to remove them with a lot of hard work and sweat in order to make the topsoil decent for planting seeds. This process certainly taught me endurance and patience.

God prepares the soil of our hearts to receive His Word through a "breaking up" process. It may come through a disaster, like an earthquake, tornado, tidal wave, fire, or flood. Often it comes through personal tragedy—sickness, a friend's death— or a disappointment. If you find yourself amid hard circumstances, God may be softening or breaking up the rocks in your soil so He can use the seed of His Word to teach you new truths.

As men, we often fight this soil preparation. We want to be in control. But we need to relax and let go, to stop fighting. We need to allow God to have His way and break up the soil for us.

Today's Action

If you're amid a life-changing event now, let go and allow God to work the soil of your life.

Prayer

Father God, thank You for loving me enough to change me into who You want me to be. Amen.

Surviving Hard Times

Do not fret because of evildoers.
Psalm 37:1

As I look at the world struggling with the results of evil, I see five ways we can depend on God's design and purpose and survive. In Psalm 37, David tells us not to fret but instead:

- *Trust God* (verse 3): Many times people will disappoint us, but God never will.
- *Do good things* (verse 3): The more good we do, the less chance evil will make an impact.
- *Delight in the Lord* (verse 4): Take delight in the things of the Lord. He promises to meet our needs.
- *Commit our way to God* (verse 5): He will be a blessing unto you.
- *Wait patiently for the Lord* (verse 7): He will overcome every situation.

The more time we spend studying God's Word and surrounding ourselves with positive influences, the less time we'll have to worry. This is how we survive hard and even evil times.

Today's Action

Look around until you see something good happening—then rejoice! Shout from the mountaintop that thing that is good.

Prayer

Father God, I thank You for all Your goodness.
I want to grow so close to You that I don't have time
or the negative because I'm so focused on the positive. Amen.

THE PROMISE OF FORGIVENESS

Who is a God like You, who pardons iniquity?
MICAH 7:18

Somehow the church hasn't done a good job of letting the world know that churches are for sinners more than they're for saints. Have you ever wondered how God could forgive your sins and all of your unrighteousness toward Him? Only through the wonder of His grace can we begin to realize the awesomeness of forgiveness. Even though we can't understand this grace, we can sit back, rejoice, and marvel at God's goodness for making us clean before Him.

The great prophet Micah acknowledged the Lord's goodness and expressed confidence in His continuing promise to forgive and bless His people. He was given this revelation long before Jesus was born into this world, lived for thirty-three years, died on the cross, and then rose from the grave. So because he lived prior to Christ, Micah wasn't able to read about Paul's triumphant telling of God's grace: No sin is so great that it cannot be forgiven.

May we all grasp the powerful promise of forgiveness!

Today's Action

Go to the throne of God and ask for His abundant grace that will forgive all of your sins.

Prayer

Father God, I'm thankful I can pray in confidence and adoration, declaring, "Who is a God like You?" Amen.

An Amazing Pronouncement

Behold, Lord, half of my possessions
I will give to the poor, and if I have defrauded anyone of anything,
I will give back four times as much.

Luke 19:8

All around the world, Christians are known for being a generous people. Many believers have given plentifully of their wealth to build schools, hospitals, universities, medical research centers, and churches.

Zacchaeus, a short tax man, shinnied up a sycamore tree to get a good look at Jesus. And through this encounter, he made the revolutionary statement in today's Scripture. This is an amazing pronouncement. Have you ever encountered the truth and went away wanting to do some great act of generosity? Well, that's how this tax man felt.

How a man feels about his money usually reflects his walk with God. Show me a stingy man, and I'll show you a man who's far away from God. But show me a giving man, and I'll show you a man who walks close to God.

Today's Action

Do you have a love and generosity that's compatible with God's unending grace to you? If so, do something today that shows that love.

Prayer

Father God, thank You for Your generosity on the cross and for setting me free. Amen.

No Job Is Too Small

He who is faithful in a very little thing is faithful also in much.
LUKE 16:10

We're so concerned about the kinds of jobs God gives us, asking:

"Is this important enough for me?"

"God certainly wouldn't want me to just empty wastebaskets [or mow the lawn, or wash the church bus, or help out at the church breakfast]."

Yet Christians who attend to these details make valuable contributions to the ministry of Christ. We must not become resistant to or weary of doing the little things, because in God's eyes, even the smallest tasks are important.

The following story illustrates my point.

As construction began on a magnificent cathedral, the archbishop in charge promised a large reward to the person who made the most important contribution to finishing the sanctuary. As the building went up, people speculated about who would win the prize. The architect? The contractor? The artisans skilled in gold, iron, brass, and glass? Perhaps the carpenter assigned to the detailed grillwork?

Because each worker did their best, the completed church was a masterpiece. But when the moment came to announce the winner, everyone was surprised. It was given to an old, poorly dressed peasant woman. What had she done? Every day, she'd faithfully carried hay to the ox that pulled the marble for the stonecutter.

If it's done for the Lord, there's no such thing as a job that's too small.

Today's Action

Consider how you can begin helping in some way, no matter how small. If you're already serving, be renewed by considering your contribution.

Prayer

Father God, help me be faithful in my service,
no matter how big or small my task. Amen.

STAND AND WALK

He said to the paralytic, "I say to you, get up,
and pick up your stretcher and go home."

LUKE 5:24

The story beginning in Luke 5:17 tells us about some men who wanted to take their friend to Jesus to be healed. The man was paralyzed, so they had to carry him on his bed. Can you imagine how the people of the city stared? But as the group arrived at the house where Jesus was teaching inside, the crowd was so large that they couldn't get close enough to Him. Someone suggested they take the bed up on the roof and lower him inside.

Can't you just hear the dialogue that might have gone on between these friends?

"We can't tear into a roof!"

"The debris will fall down on top of Jesus!"

"Who will fix the roof when we're finished?"

Fortunately for the paralyzed man, someone took control. The group found the way up to the roof and removed some of its tiles, then lowered the man through the hole, perhaps by tying ropes to the corners of his bed. And when He saw the man, Jesus looked at him and first said, "Your sins are forgiven."

These friends didn't waste time debating who would fix the roof; they just earnestly wanted their friend to be healed and did what was necessary. And Jesus was open to the unorthodox way the paralyzed man was brought to Him. He wanted to be asked for healing, and the paralyzed man was obedient to His command when He said, "Rise...and go home." Luke 5:25 says, "At once he rose up before them, and took up what he had been lying on, and went home glorifying God."

Today's Action
Stand and walk to wherever Jesus is telling you to go.

Prayer
Father God, may my heart be obedient to Your commands.
Amen.

THANK GOD

Blessed be the LORD,
because He has heard the voice of my supplication.
PSALM 28:6

In a seacoast town where great ships set sail to cross the mighty ocean stood a small church. The pastor printed a year-end statistical report for his congregation, and the parishioners noted an unusual entry: "Missing at sea: 9." The members didn't know of any of their number being lost at sea, so someone asked the pastor what he meant.

"Well," he replied, "during the year, eleven of you asked me to pray for family or friends going out to sea. Because I heard only two of you thank the Lord for their safe return, I assume the remaining nine are still missing!"

We often forget to give thanks when God answers our prayers. But we should be quick to show our appreciation, because our heavenly Father is pleased when we thank Him. When our Lord was on earth, He lifted His voice to His Father and expressed thanks for food (John 6:11), the simplicity of the gospel (Matthew 11:25), and answered prayer (John 11:41).

We should never forget to give God our thanks.

Today's Action

Thank God for an answered prayer.

Prayer

Father God, I thank You over and over
for Your goodness and provision. Amen.

Governed by Love

*Take care that this liberty of yours does not
somehow become a stumbling block to the weak.*

1 Corinthians 8:9

I'm often asked what Christians can and cannot do. In the book of 1 Corinthians, Paul discussed whether Christians could eat meat offered to the idols of pagan gods. God's Word gave the sign that it would be okay, but for Paul to do what was permitted could cause a weaker Christian to stumble. In dealing with his conscience, then, he stopped eating the meat.

Have you ever faced a similar dilemma? Have you ever chosen not to do something that's permissible because you don't want to be a stumbling block to someone else's walk with the Lord—especially a new Christian's? Paul chose not to insist on his own rights, realizing that liberty must be controlled and governed by love. This is a basic principle we must live by, because a fellow believer might act contrary to their own conscience based on how they see us live.

When we love the Lord, we will also love our brothers and sisters. Love does limit liberty to promote the maturing of our fellow believers, but when we're governed by love, we'll always find freedom.

Today's Action

Are any of your liberties hindering a fellow Christian from maturing in the Lord? If so, consider how you can change—then do it.

Prayer

Father God, help me examine my actions and evaluate my liberties so I can love my brother or sister more. Amen.

Hear the Bells

My sheep listen to my voice.
John 10:27 niv

A young man from a West Texas farm community received a football scholarship from a small college in Texas. He was excited about this new adventure as he packed his bags for school, and after his mother's hugs and tears, she asked her son to make her one promise: "Attend church every Sunday while you're away from home." With no hesitation, he assured his mama he would honor that request.

After settling into his dorm, he met several incoming freshmen he liked. But these young men had few if any spiritual interests. One of the boys came from a wealthy farm family nearby, and he invited his new friends to come home with him for the weekend to hunt and fish. The small-town farm boy said, "Yes. That will be fun."

On Sunday morning, as they mounted their horses to ride to where the hunting and fishing were good, the young man heard bells ringing from a nearby church. Then as they rode toward their day's adventure, he heard a fainter ringing of the church bells. Going farther and farther, he again heard the church bells ring, but this time their sound was very faint. He stopped his horse and told his host he had to go back. He had to attend church.

The host said, "We don't have to go to church today. Let's go on, and I'll go to church with you next week."

But the young man replied, "No, I must go back while I can still hear the bells!"

Are you in that young man's situation? You once heard God's voice, but it's become faint because you moved away from Him? If so, your conscience might be calling out, *Go back while you can still hear the voice of God!*

If you feel far away from God, guess who moved? Return to Him before you can no longer hear His voice calling you.

Today's Action

How well do you hear the bells ringing? If their sound isn't strong, turn back to your first love. Listen to God's voice.

Prayer

Father God, continue to ring the bells loud and clear. I never want to stop hearing Your call. May everything that could hinder me from hearing Your voice be silenced. Amen.

No Visa Required

Our citizenship is in heaven, from which also
we eagerly wait for a Savior, the Lord Jesus Christ.
PHILIPPIANS 3:20

When I was in the manufacturing business many years ago, my wife, Emilie, and I had the privilege of going on an awards trip to Spain and North Africa. What a thrilling experience! We applied for our passports and visas, and in about four weeks we were cleared to take this great adventure.

While in Spain, we traveled on the first of May, which was sometimes a turbulent "labor day" for that country. Wherever we went we were met with guards carrying automatic rifles. They anticipated possible rioting and were careful to make sure everything was in order when they inspected our paperwork.

The next day we sailed to Algiers in North Africa, where the immigration authorities requested that we drop our passports and visas into a bag so they could clear us as a group. Emilie and I were hesitant to do this, because our passports were our proof of American citizenship. So we were grateful when they were returned with the proper stamps.

It won't be like that when we enter heaven. Christians are honored citizens there. When our time comes, we won't have to worry about getting in. No guards, no passports, no visas, and no border crossings are required. We'll be welcomed into heaven because our citizenship papers are already there.

Today's Action

If you're not sure of your citizenship in heaven, turn to the Lord
Jesus Christ today (John 3:16).

Prayer

*Lord Jesus, I so appreciate what You did on the cross so I can
gain access to heaven. Amen.*

The Worst Day Fishing

Confirm for us the work of our hands;
yes, confirm the work of our hands.

Psalm 90:17

Saint Francis of Assisi was hoeing his garden when someone asked him what he would do if he suddenly learned he would die before sunset that very day. "I would finish hoeing my garden," he replied. Saint Francis definitely understood the worth of his hands.

Yet we men sometimes struggle with knowing the worth of our hands. We debate with ourselves about what our work's worth is:

"Am I in the right profession?"

"I'm restless in what I do; I tend to want to change jobs every few years."

"I don't find fulfillment in my work."

A lot of men feel trapped in what they do. A fisherman once said, "The worst day of fishing is better than the best day at work."

In the past, a believer's work had spiritual significance. They worked unto the Lord. Their craftsmanship reflected upon God, and they took great pride in producing the end product. But for too many, our work ethic has changed over the years.

We need to return to that mindset—seeing our jobs as a testimony to our Savior.

Today's Action

If your job is drudgery to you, change your attitude toward it—
or switch to a job you can get excited about.

Prayer

Father God, thank You for giving me hands to work.
May my work reflect my love for You. Amen.

A Way of Escape

We do not have a high priest who cannot sympathize with our weaknesses, but One who has been tempted in all things as we are, yet without sin.

Hebrews 4:15

One of the great offerings of grace is that we can go directly to God without a high priest. We can enter into God's abode without the blood of animals and peace offerings.

When Jesus walked on this earth, He was tempted just like we are. Many forks in the road required daily decision-making for Him to stay on the high road. He was a man just like us in every way but two—He never yielded to temptation, and He never fell into sin. He did, however, experience the need to wait on God for guidance.

When we call on Jesus for help in our difficult periods of life, He's always in a position to state, "Yes, I know what you're experiencing—I've been there." He can identify with how hard it can be to live for God in this fallen world. Isn't it great to know that He's experienced what we're now experiencing?

In 1 Corinthians 10:13, Paul gave us a great promise: When we're tempted, God, in His faithfulness, will give us a way to escape so we can endure it.

Today's Action
When you're facing difficulties in life, seek God's way of escape.

Prayer
Father God, please help me when I stumble, and be merciful to me, a sinner. Amen.

Entering Heaven's Gate

Things which eye has not seen and ear has not heard,
and which have not entered the heart of man,
all that God has prepared for those who love Him.
1 Corinthians 2:9

Have you ever pondered what heaven will be like? From the time I was a child, I've often given thought to what life after this present existence will be. One thing is for sure: God, Jesus, and the Holy Spirit will be there. C.S. Lewis said that while we're living on this earth, we're on the wrong side of the door. But he also added, "All the leaves of the New Testament are rustling with the rumor it will not always be so."[12]

Knowing Jesus as our personal Savior and believing and accepting what He did on the cross for our sins gives us entrance into eternity. We won't enter heaven's gate because of our own good character or service; we'll see our Savior only because of our faith in His supreme sacrifice on the cross.

When we reach heaven, we'll truly understand what 1 Corinthians 2:9 tells us: God will open the gates of heaven to those who open their hearts to Him.

Today's Action

Contemplate what heaven will be like.

Prayer

Father God, prepare my heart to look forward to the day when I will be with You in heaven. Amen.

Entering the Unknown

You have not passed this way before.

Joshua 3:4

Some people are thrill seekers. The faster the blood flows through their veins, the more alive they feel. These people live on the edge. To them, the normalcy of life is boring, so they're always pushing the envelope.

My own style is a little more on the conservative side, so I tend to play it safe. But many situations require a lot of faith on our part because we've never "passed this way before." Unknown situations make us uneasy. But talking to Christian friends, reading Scripture, and praying will give us the insights we need so we can handle life's difficulties.

Much like Moses did when he led the nation of Israel out of Egypt through the Red Sea, Joshua had to lead his people across the Jordan River into the Holy Land. The priests among them had never had such a faith experience, but they had to first put their feet into the water and then stand on the bed before the parted waters flowed back. What faith had to be exhibited when entering the unknown—a way not passed before!

Today's Action

Contemplate the faith-stretching situations in your life. Are you depending on God for guidance? Even though you may not have passed this way before, have faith that God will see you through.

Prayer

Father God, give me the heart to have extreme faith in extreme situations. Amen.

A True Legacy

What do these stones mean to you?

Joshua 4:6

Our country's many monuments help us remember what great events took place either in a particular spot or nationwide. We never want to let future generations forget what great sacrifices were made in order for them to have freedom.

Joshua built a monument of stones so the Israelite children of the future would ask, "What do these stones mean?" Then the people could say to them, "'Because the waters of the Jordan were cut off before the ark of the covenant of the LORD; when it crossed the Jordan, the waters of the Jordan were cut off.' So these stones shall become a memorial to the sons of Israel forever" (verses 6-7 NASB).

As a father and grandfather, I often wonder what my legacy will be when the Lord calls me home. Will my family remember me as a man who built his life with hay and stubble (1 Corinthians 3:13 KJV), or will they remember me as a man of God who represented the true virtues of life? Each day I find myself continuing to make choices that require commitment to God. I trust that my legacy will reflect the man I've tried to become.

Today's Action

How would you answer this question: "What do these 'stones' mean to you?"

Prayer

Father God, may my monument reflect that I am Your child.
Amen.

The Book of Books

Our gospel did not come to you in word only, but also in power.
1 Thessalonians 1:5

We so take for granted our present-day Bible and its many translations. But in the first century, the gospel was transmitted verbally while it was put into written form. Believers throughout time have proclaimed the truths of Scripture around the world—even in some regions that don't take kindly to Christianity. And I believe the Bible has become the number one bestseller because God's Word brings salvation and hope to people of every station in life.

The broad influence of this Book of books was expressed beautifully by American clergyman and author Henry Van Dyke:

> Born in the East and clothed in oriental form and imagery, the Bible walks the ways of all the world with familiar feet, and enters land after land to find its own everywhere. It has learned to speak in hundreds of languages to the heart of man. It comes into the palace to tell the monarch that he is the servant of the Most High, and into the cottage to assure the peasant that he is the son of God.[13]

Kings and peasants have believed, nations have been altered, and cultures have improved because of the Bible's message. Yes, the Bible has indeed made a difference wherever it's gone.

The Scriptures can change your life if you read them, digest their concepts, learn their truths, and apply them to your life. Great light has shone from this Book—even in the world's darkest hours.

Today's Action

Take a moment to thank God for giving us the people who have fervently and accurately translated the Bible into many languages.

Prayer

Father God, help me respect the contents of Your Holy Bible and apply its precepts to my life. Amen.

A Rich and Pleasing Intimacy

May he kiss me with the kisses of his mouth!
For your love is better than wine.
Song of Songs 1:2

The Bible's book called Song of Songs (or Song of Solomon) portrays the pattern of married love as God intended it to be. This dynamic book is about the marriage between the king of Israel and a lovely country girl he met in his vineyards. This is not a fantasy storybook. It presents true-to-life episodes dealing with real-life situations so that thousands of years later we may know this marriage truly pleased and honored God. If you're a first-time reader, you may be surprised to find such expressions of love in the Bible.

Song of Songs illustrates the need for emotional, spiritual, and physical give-and-take for rich and meaningful sexual intimacy. Men and women are uniquely different in how they respond sexually, so you must explore the mysterious and unusual ways of pleasing a wife. Remember that most if not all women tend to respond to sex more in terms of caring, sharing, hugging, and kissing than men do. Think of each other, put each other first in your relationship, and enjoy a rich and pleasing intimacy.

Today's Action

If you're married, kiss your wife and tell her you love her. Ask what you can do to make your intimacy more pleasurable for her.

Prayer

Father God, through Your Word, teach me what it means to be a loving husband. Amen.

Making Time for God

I shall call upon [the Lord] as long as I live.
Psalm 116:2

Are you doing what's important in your day—or only what's urgent? We all make choices, and people tend to do what they want to do. But when we don't make time for God in our day—when we don't make time for the most important relationship in our lives—we're probably not making the best choices.

God greatly desires to spend time alone with you. After all, you are His child (John 1:12; Galatians 3:26). He created you, He loves you, and He gave His only Son for your salvation. So make it a priority to spend time with Him daily. There's no single right time or correct place; your meeting time and place with Him will vary according to the season of your life and the schedule you're juggling. You can talk to God when you're standing in line, waiting for an appointment, eating lunch alone, or stopped at a red light. You don't have to make an appointment to ask Him for something you need or to thank Him for something you've received.

Where and when you meet God may change, but meeting with Him alone each day should be a constant in your life. What should you do in your planned time alone with God? You can read and meditate on His Word, and you can spend time in prayer. Talk to Him as you would talk to your earthly parents or to a special friend who loves you.

God always loves hearing from you, and He's interested in everything that happens to you. He always makes time for you, so be sure to always make time for Him.

Today's Action

If you're not already spending time with God each day, decide to try it for one month. Then set aside a time and stick to it.

Prayer

Father God, thank You for being within the sound of my voice and only a thought's distance away. Amen.

Show Your Love

Do you love Me?
John 21:15

Our Lord looks for an "I love You" from His children that's backed up by action. When He asked Peter, "Do you love Me?" He wasn't satisfied with a casual, "Sure, Lord, You know I do!" Jesus asked this question of Peter more than once, and each time He responded to His disciple's reply by saying, in effect, "Peter, if you love Me, care for those I care for. Peter, if you love Me, follow Me." With each response Jesus was telling Peter, "If you love Me, tend My lambs and tend My sheep." In other words, if there's love, there's action that reflects that love. Jesus said, in essence, "If you love Me, do something to show your love for Me."

What would you say if the Lord asked if you loved Him? Would you answer, "Yes, Lord, I love You"? Oh, may our words delight the Father's heart because they come from obedient children—and may we show Him our love! The best proof of love for God is love for one another.

Today's Action

How are your relationships? Do any need repair? If so, now is a good time to straighten out any difficulty you're having with a friend, family member, or anyone else.

Prayer

Jesus, give me direction
to follow Your command
to tend Your sheep. Amen.

A Common Commitment

Then Isaac...took Rebekah, and she became his wife, and he loved her.
Genesis 24:67

Isaac was not a dynamic man like his father, Abraham. Yet his singular love for Rebekah stands in sharp contrast to the other patriarchs of his time, who had concubines and many wives. Nothing in Scripture suggests that Isaac ever followed that practice. He's portrayed as a kind, loving, faithful husband.

Whenever my wife, Emilie, and I met couples who'd been married forty-plus years, we loved to hear their stories of courtship and marriage. They all had some rocky roads along the way, but they shared a common commitment—they stuck it out. They expressed their joy by saying, "I'm so glad we endured the rough times. Now we're truly receiving God's blessing for our obedience."

True love endures in spite of difficulties. Paul said, "Love never fails" (1 Corinthians 13:8). Love doesn't depend on the continuance of pleasing qualities in the loved one.

Even the best couples go through difficult times. If you're married, create a deep desire in your heart and soul to look after the welfare of your wife. Let it grow more enduring the older you become, and grow closer to the Lord as you deepen your commitment to each other.

Today's Action

If you're married, do something that shows your wife how important her welfare is to you.

Prayer

Father God, thank You for giving me my wife, and help me love and care for her. Amen.

Serving with Humility

*Have this attitude in yourselves
which was also in Christ Jesus.*

Philippians 2:5

Each time I blow it, Philippians 2:5 crosses my mind and leads me to a prayer that goes something like this: *Thank You, Lord, for revealing to me that I've still got a long way to go before I have Your attitude—one of humility.* Yes, the Lord continually gives me the opportunity to realize that I need to work on developing humbleness.

In this world of social media and self-promotion, it's easy to become confused about what genuine humility is. But having the mind and heart and attitude of Christ is a good start. Philippians 2:3 says, "Do nothing out of selfish ambition or vain conceit, but in humility consider others better than yourself" (NIV).

As we serve others, we need to do it with a right heart—seeking to please God, not desiring any glory or honor for ourselves.

Today's Action

In what three capacities or organizations would you be willing to serve? Step forward and volunteer your services in one of these areas.

Prayer

Father God, I need to develop humility
and learn to give myself away to others.
Teach me to be humble. Amen.

Drink Deeply

If any man is thirsty, let him come to Me and drink.

John 7:37

A little girl from a poor family was in the hospital when a nurse brought her a glass filled to the brim with milk. This was the first time the girl had been given an entire glass of milk for herself; she usually had to share with her brothers and sisters. And when the nurse returned to the girl's room, she found the glass still full.

"Why didn't you drink it?" the nurse asked.

"You didn't tell me how deep I could drink," the little girl replied.

The nurse fought back tears. "Drink all of it," she said tenderly. "This whole glass is just for you."

We're told if we wait to drink until we feel thirsty, we've already started to dehydrate. That's the way it is with God. In our timidity, we tend to take just a small sip of the water He has to offer. But Jesus tells us to drink deeply. Don't wait until a problem arises before you start praying and spending time in God's Word. Connect with God during the good times so you'll know how to pray in the hard times.

The moment a spiritual need arises, invite God to fill it. When you're on the verge of losing your temper, pray, *Your patience, Lord.* When you're alone, pray, *Your presence, Lord.* When you're anxious, pray, *Your peace, Lord.* And when you're tempted by lustful thoughts, pray, *Your purity, Lord.*

Today's Action

Go to Jesus and drink deeply of His Everlasting Water.

Prayer

Father God, thank You for letting me drink freely from Your cup of life. Amen.

Overcoming Rejection

Of His fullness we have all received,
and grace upon grace.

John 1:16

Little hurts as much as rejection. When have you experienced rejection in your life? Did it come from a special girl in high school, a failed college exam, a withheld promotion, a home loan not approved? How did you react to this rejection? Were you hurt? Angry? To whom did you go for comfort?

We can always go to Jesus when we're rebuffed. He who was nailed to the cross knows all about rejection. Jesus shouted to God in heaven, "My God, my God, why have you forsaken me?" (Matthew 27:46 NIV). Yet despite all of the rejection Jesus experienced, He never abandoned the mission God gave Him, never retaliated against those who scorned Him, and responded in love to those who tried to offend Him.

Jesus gives us His grace to help us when we're hurting. These promises are for us:

- "Never will I leave you" (Hebrews 13:5 NIV).
- Praise be to God...who comforts us in all our troubles (2 Corinthians 1:3-4).
- You were marked in him with a seal (Ephesians 1:13).

Today's Action

Make a list of times you've experienced rejection. What has God taught you through each of these events?

Prayer

Father God, help me use rejections to become more like You.
Amen.

Fear or Love?

*Everyone who has left houses or brothers
or sisters or father or mother or children or farms
for My name's sake, will receive many times as much.*

MATTHEW 19:29

Why do we do what we do? Through the years, I've asked myself again and again, *Why do I serve? What is my motivation for speaking, writing, giving to the church, being a father and a grandfather, and loving my wife and family?* To put it more bluntly, *What will I get as a result of my efforts?*

Peter said to Jesus, "We have left everything to follow You! What then will there be for us?" (Matthew 29:27 NIV). Jesus answered Peter's question and told him—and us—the benefits of serving God and His kingdom:

- We will receive a hundred times as much as we give up (NIV).
- We will inherit eternal life.
- Many who are last will be first.

These rewards are gracious and generous, but are you letting them motivate your service to God? Or do you, like many people, serve God because you think He will punish you if you don't?

My own list of blessings continues on and on, each item reminding me that God does indeed take care of His people when they sacrifice to serve Him and choose love over fear.

Today's Action

List at least ten of your blessings, then consider what they show you about God.

Prayer

Father God, show me my true motivation
for serving You. Amen.

The Command to Love

*You shall love the LORD your God
with all your heart and with all your
soul and with all your might.*

DEUTERONOMY 6:5

Jesus Christ called loving God with all your heart, soul, mind, and strength the first and greatest commandment (Mark 12:30). And today's verse, along with Matthew 22:36-38, talks about three basic loves—love of God, love of neighbor, and love of self. What a difference we would make in the world if we consistently loved in these three ways! Clearly, the command to love is important to God.

As we try to remain constantly aware of God's command, how do we live out these three loves? In Ephesians 5:19-21, we get a small glimpse on how to love this way. If we

- love ourselves, we will speak and sing words of joy. We will make music in our hearts for the Lord.
- love God, we will always give thanks for all things in the name of our Lord Jesus Christ. Positive words will flow from our lips unto God.
- love our neighbors, we will be willing to allow other people's needs to take precedence over our own.

These are great actions for our Christian growth, but we can't do them in our own power. We must rely on God, and we must start by loving Him with all our heart, soul, strength, and mind. Then we can begin following His command to love others.

Today's Action

Write down several specific ways you can love God.

Prayer

Father God, help me better understand what kind of love You want me to have. Amen.

GOD CONTINUALLY PROVIDES

Do not be afraid, for am I in God's place?
You meant evil against me but God meant it for good
in order to bring about this present result.

GENESIS 50:20-21

The story of Joseph and his family, which begins in Genesis 37, is a terrific example of how God provides for us. In brief summary, Jacob favored his son Joseph. Extremely jealous, Joseph's brothers plotted against him and sold him as a slave. But God was with Joseph, who ended up in Egypt and a trusted servant of Pharaoh.

Now, Joseph was Pharaoh's grain overseer, so when Jacob sent his sons to Egypt to buy grain during a famine, they encountered Joseph. But they didn't recognize him. Genesis 50:19-20 shares Joseph's words as he revealed himself to his brothers. And then he said what they did against him, God meant for good. The wisdom that "God causes all things to work together for the good to those who love God" (Romans 8:28) is demonstrated by this story.

Yes, we can trust that God allows even evildoers to play a part in developing us into what He wants us to be. Trust Him for every event in your life.

Today's Action

Are you experiencing a challenging or difficult situation now? If so, consider how God might be working in it for good.

Prayer

Father God, help me trust You more in all the circumstances of my life. Amen.

Jesus Weeps with You

You have taken account of my wanderings;
put my tears in Your bottle. Are they not in Your book?
Psalm 56:8

David was so amazed that God was attentive to every detail of his life—even down to the awareness of the tears he shed. To think that our great God takes notice even of our tears and saves them as jewels! He promises that "they that sow in tears shall reap in joy" (Psalm 126:5 kjv). Our tears will be turned into pearls, precious gems for God. And they're posted in His book of remembrance, for He doesn't forget our heartaches.

John 11:35 declares that "Jesus wept." Yes, Jesus weeps when we weep. Albert Smith defined tears as "the safety valve of the heart when too much pressure is laid on."[14]

There are various types of tears:

- tears of love
- tears of exhortation and forgiveness
- tears of compassion
- tears of spiritual desire and hope

But also:
- tears of sorrow
- tears of joy

It's comforting to know that when you're sad, Jesus weeps for you and promises to turn your tears into joy.

Today's Action

Don't be afraid to shed tears when your heart is filled with sadness. Be willing to release them.

Prayer

Father God, let me be open enough with my family that I can show them my emotions—even my tears. Amen.

A Kindred Spirit

There is a friend
who sticks closer than a brother.
PROVERBS 18:24

I often wonder why some people are attracted to others. Because of common interests, past experiences, physical attributes, having children who are friends with another family's kids, or attending the same church? What bonds people together?

As I consider the many friends I have, I sense it's a little of all of the above. My friends come from various backgrounds, religions, economic levels, and educational achievement. One common strand, however, seems to run through most of these friendships: We have a kindred spirit in the Lord.

The writer of today's proverb gives a warning in the first part of verse 24: "A man of many friends comes to ruin." When I first read that, I was confused. I thought, *But we're to have a lot of friends, so why this warning?* But as I thought about it, another idea came to me. The writer was stressing that too many friends chosen indiscriminately will bring trouble, but a genuine friend sticks with you through thick and thin. When we use this criterion for a friend, we begin to thin the acquaintance ranks down to those who are truly our friends.

Without a doubt, I know that several of my friends would be with me no matter what the circumstance, what the day of the week, or what the time of day or night I needed help. I call these my "2 a.m. friends." You never know when you'll need a friend like this.

I've also found that those who have friends are friendly themselves, going out of their way to be a friend. In order to have friends, one must be a friend. Friendship-making is a skill we need to teach our children—and keep working on ourselves. When we choose friends who follow the Lord and show kindness to others, we've found our kindred spirits.

Today's Action

Write someone a note expressing how much you appreciate their friendship.

Prayer

Father God, You've given me some wonderful friends. I thank You for what they mean to me. Amen.

A Special Friendship

Make my joy complete by being
of the same mind, maintaining the same love,
united in spirit, intent on one purpose.

PHILIPPIANS 2:2

Paul wrote about the discord within the church in the book of Philippians, and then he made a statement kind of like Clint Eastwood's famous movie line, "Go ahead, make my day." Paul said, "Make my joy complete"—by getting along with each other. Stop bickering and backbiting. Be friends.

Did you know some research indicates friendly people live longer than the general population? Friendship is also the launching pad for every love, so it spills into the other important relationships of life. Friendship is the beginning of all levels of intimacy—with a spouse, with parents, with children, with everyone we encounter. Philippians 2:2 encourages us to heal our relationships and start getting along if we want to experience special friendships. Few of us are privileged to be able to share our innermost thoughts with someone.

"But how do I develop such friendships?" you may ask. Follow these basic principles with both the people you want to be friends and friends you already have:

- Make friendship a top priority.
- Be willing to take a risk and be transparent.
- Express your care for them.

- Learn and exhibit the language of love and friendship.
- Give them room to be who they are.

Today's Action

Do something for a friend that lets them know they're your friend.

Prayer

Father God, I truly want to have special friends in my life.
Help me start getting along better with others today
and develop the friendships I desire. Amen.

Who Moved Away?

Behold, like the clay in the potter's hand,
so are you in My hand.
Jeremiah 18:6

When our son, Brad, was in elementary school, his teacher asked everyone in the class to shape a lump of clay into something useful or artistic. Brad molded and shaped his clay with his small hands, and we proudly displayed the red dinosaur-type sculpture he brought home on our bookshelf.

Later, in high school, Brad enrolled in a ceramics class. His first pieces were crooked and misshapen, but as time went on, he made some pieces of real art—vases, pots, pitchers, and various other kinds of pottery. But many of the pieces of clay Brad threw on the pottery wheel took a different direction than he intended. He would work and work to reshape the clay, and sometimes he had to start all over to make it exactly the way he wanted it to be.

With each one of us, God has, so to speak, taken a handful of clay to make us exactly who He wants us to be. He is the Master Potter, and we are the vessels in His hands. As He shapes us on the Potter's wheel, He reworks us on the inside and the outside. He says, "I am with you. I am the Lord of your life, and I will build within you a strong foundation based upon My Word."

The Master Potter also uses the circumstances of life to shape us. When things go wrong, the Potter can seem far away. We may feel forgotten by God, so we pull away from Him because we think He "let us down." As time passes, God seems even more distant, and it seems like the Potter's work is put on hold. But God said, "I will not fail you or forsake you" (Joshua 1:5).

When we feel far from God, we need to remember that He didn't abandon us. We're the ones who moved away. He's always ready to continue molding us into the people He intends us to be.

Today's Action

Give back to God what you took from Him because you didn't feel you could trust Him—whether that's control over your family, your finances, or anything else.

Prayer

Father God, help me trust You more each day as I give back what belongs to You. Amen.

Be Prepared Before the Storm

He will be the stability of your times,
a wealth of salvation, wisdom, and knowledge;
the fear of the LORD is his treasure.

ISAIAH 33:6

In this crazy world of ours, I'm always losing my foundation. I place my trust in politicians, and they fail me. I look to the heroes of the sports world, and they let me down. I purchase a sure-win stock, and it loses value. Even the pillars of the church can let me down. "Where, oh where is my stability?" cries out the modern man. Everywhere he looks, he's deceived. He sees changes on the horizon and isn't sure what lies ahead.

Even though our stability is shaken in the present, in Isaiah 33:6, God promises that He will always be the same—He'll never waver. When the storms of life hit, we can always rely on Him to see us through safely.

Times of instability come to all of us. Even if our lives are stable today, tomorrow we may not be as fortunate. Isn't it wonderful to know that when change comes, we can go to God's Word to find the strength to see us through another situation? Let's not wait for the storm to hit before we seek Scripture that comforts and directs us. Let's prepare ourselves for when these days appear.

Today's Action

Do you see any stormy changes coming? If so, what are they?
What Scripture will help you get through them?

Prayer

Father God, prepare our hearts with Scripture that will see us
through the stormy changes of life. Amen.

A Reverence for God

The fear of the LORD is the beginning of wisdom;
a good understanding have all those who do His commandments;
His praise endures forever.

Psalm 111:10

The fear of the Lord" is a reverence for God expressed in submission to His will (Job 28:28; Ecclesiastes 12:13; Proverbs 9:10; 15:33). It's also the starting point for the essence of wisdom. Wisdom isn't acquired by following a mechanical formula but through developing a right relationship with God. It seems that following God's principles should be the obvious conclusion of our thankfulness for all He's done for us.

But in today's world, many people have lost sight of the concept of fearing God. The soft side of Christianity has preached only the "love of God." We haven't balanced the scale by teaching the other side of justice—fear, anger, wrath, and punishment. Just because some in church pulpits don't teach it doesn't make it less of a reality. As with involvement with drugs, alcohol, lust, and envy, we must respect the consequences of our actions or we'll be destroyed by their side effects.

We gain wisdom when we have a proper reverence for God. Only then will we be able to obey His precepts and stay away from the fire of temptation.

Today's Action

As you go about your day, exhibit a new respect for your all-powerful God.

Prayer

Father God, fill me with an awesome respect for You.
I want to be obedient to Your precepts. Amen.

Two Things to Do

Prove yourselves doers of the word,
and not merely hearers who [deceive] themselves.
James 1:22

Susannah Wesley once said you do two things with the gospel: You believe it, and you live it. I often think living it is harder than believing it. Our children look at how we live our everyday lives more than they think about mere belief, and that means our example to them is powerful.

Our wisdom in guiding our children through their growing-up years is one of the best measures of how much we love and value them. Moms are extremely important, but the love and worth kids receive from their dads is vital for them to stay on course.

If you're a father, you won't be able to sell your kids on a double standard when it comes to the important issues of life. They'll be more willing to follow what you do and what you believe than what you say.

No one else can be as good a father to your children as you can. You're helping to build tomorrow's future. Remember to believe God's Word—and then live it.

Today's Action

Show your children who you are and what you believe by what you do, not just by what you say.

Prayer

Father God, let me realize the magnitude of being a father, and help me live out my beliefs. Amen.

Restoration and Refuge

His name will be called
Wonderful Counselor, Mighty God,
Eternal Father, Prince of Peace.

Isaiah 9:6

As we're told in Isaiah 9:6, Christ has many names. But what do you think of when you hear the name Jesus? Miracles? Salvation? Peace? Purpose? Joy? Power? Hope? All of these things and more? There's indeed something about that name.

The fact that Christ lives today gives us hope and peace. As Isaiah wrote, "Of the increase of his government of peace there will be no end" (9:7 NIV). Life brings sorrow, broken hearts, health problems, financial difficulties, and many other hardships. But Jesus, who is God, gives us peace and hope for those times. So allow yourself to depend on Jesus in times of difficulty and find refuge and restoration in Him.

It helps some people to visualize putting all their problems and worries in a box, sealing the lid, laying it at Jesus' feet, and then walking away, never turning back. It also helps to realize that probably 80 percent of what we worry about never happens anyway—and we can let Jesus take the remaining 20 percent. In response, He'll give back to you 100 percent of His life and peace. In fact, He did that already when He died on the cross of Calvary.

Jesus. There's indeed something about that name—and in Him you'll find restoration, refuge, and exactly what you need for today.

Today's Action

Praise Jesus for who He is. Then reel off ten blessings you're thankful for.

Prayer

Father God, in each of Jesus' names in Scripture,
please help me discover who You are. Amen.

A Formula for Life

Seek first His Kingdom and His righteousness;
and all these things shall be added to you.
Matthew 6:33

We live in an anxious society, and many of us are more worried about tomorrow than today. We bypass all of today's contentment because of what might happen in the future. And in Matthew 6:31, we read that the early Christians, like some of us, worried about even basic needs. They asked questions like:

- "What shall we eat?"
- "What shall we drink?"
- "What shall we wear?"

We're also often anxious and overwhelmed with too many things to do. Life offers many good choices for how to spend our time, but we have only twenty-four hours each day. How are we to use them effectively and without anxiety?

In Matthew 6:34, Jesus tells the people (and us), "Do not be anxious for tomorrow; for tomorrow will care for itself." Why? Because He's already given the formula for establishing the right priorities of life in the previous verse: "Seek first His Kingdom and His righteousness; and all these things shall be added to you" (verse 33).

When we seek first God's kingdom and then His righteousness, not only do we not have to worry about our needs, but our days take shape and we can say yes we'll do that or no we won't do this. When we set priorities, we determine what's important, what isn't, and how much time we're willing to give each activity.

The Bible gives us helpful guidelines for setting priorities:

- Time for our personal relationship with God (Matthew 6:33; Philippians 3:8).
- Time for home and family (Genesis 2:24; Psalm 127:3; 1 Timothy 3:2-5).
- Time for work (1 Thessalonians 4:11-12).
- Time for ministry and community activities (Colossians 3:17).

Don't be afraid to say no to certain things. If you've established Matthew 6:33 as one of the key verses in your life and follow the formula, you can often quickly decide whether an opportunity will help you seek God's kingdom and His righteousness. You'll begin to major in the big things of life and not get bogged down by minor issues or situations.

Today's Action
Say no to something that sounds good but doesn't fit your goals.

Prayer
Father God, help me discern Your will so I'll know
when to say yes and when to say no. Amen.

You Have Talents!

Well done, good and faithful servant!
You have been faithful with a few things;
I will put you in charge of many things.
Come and share your master's happiness.

Matthew 25:21 niv

God calls us to faithfully use our talents for Him. What talents has He given you? Too often we think of talents as fully developed abilities, but only as we cultivate our talents do they become mature. Furthermore, we must be willing to risk using our talents.

Consider what God is specifically saying to you in the "talent" parable Jesus told in Matthew 25:14-30. The first two servants were willing to take a risk. Not only did they receive a 100 percent return for their efforts, but their master praised them (see today's verse). Note that despite their different talents and abilities, the two servants received the same reward, indicating that God requires us to be faithful in using our abilities, whatever they are. If you want to be successful in God's eyes, you must first be faithful with the responsibilities He's given you. Then He'll put you in charge of many things.

Do people tell you you're good at something, but you just shrug it off? Do you think no one could be blessed by your gifts and talents? God's Word tells you to take the risk. Volunteer for that position, write that book, sign up for that class, offer to help with that project. Listen to God as He calls you to a life of adventure using the gifts He's given you.

Also, look at what happens when someone chooses not to use their talents. The third servant was afraid. Unwilling to take a risk with his one talent, he buried it in the ground. Then because there wasn't a return on his "investment," this third servant was condemned for his sloth and indifference.

Are you burying your talents? God will hold you responsible for what you do with them—and with your life. He wants you to take the risk of using the talents He's given you. You'll be amazed at what God can do. And one day you'll be blessed when you hear Him say, "Well done, good and faithful servant!"

Today's Action

Consider one way you can step out, take a risk, and use your talents.

Prayer

Father God, I'm nervous about taking this step, but You've promised You won't let me fall. I take You on Your word. Amen.

The Peacemaker

If a house is divided against itself,
that house will not be able to stand.

Mark 3:25

A house divided against itself cannot stand," Abraham Lincoln said in his speech accepting his nomination to the United States Senate. Then he said, "Either the opponents of slavery, will arrest the further spread of it, and place it where the public mind shall rest in the belief that it is in course of ultimate extinction, or its advocates will push it forward till it shall become alike lawful in all the states, old as well as new—North as well as South."[15]

Lincoln's stand against slavery and for the equality of all people resulted in his defeat in the Senate election, but he responded philosophically: "Though I now sink out of view, and shall be forgotten, I believe I have made some marks which will tell for the cause of civil liberty long after I am gone."[16] Well, Lincoln certainly didn't "sink out of view"! Later, as president of the United States, he worked to bring together those who had been at war and labored to heal the hurts that had divided the nation.

Many families today are divided and need to be brought together. And many hurts in families need to be healed. Perhaps such division exists in your family. If so, the warning in today's Scripture is for you. If a family remains divided, it will collapse.

What can you do to help bring unity to your family? What can you do to help healing enter your home? Whatever steps you decide to take, you'll need a lot of patience and many prayers. As you seek God's blessing on your attempts to rebuild your home, ask Him to give you wisdom and understanding.

It will take time to rebuild what's been destroyed by division, so don't expect instant results. But if you're a peacemaker who's willing to walk by faith, not by sight, and pray earnestly for unity each step of the way, God will bring unity to your situation.

Today's Action

Reach out and be a peacemaker someplace you see division, especially if it's in your own home.

Prayer

Father God, as I attempt to be a peacemaker, go before me and heal the wounds that prevail. Amen.

Honored by God

Noah found favor in the eyes of the LORD...
Thus Noah did; according to all that God had commanded him.
GENESIS 6:8, 22

If you were to glance at today's news stories, you'd probably find one about someone being honored for something they did. It seems that accomplishments in government, sports, medicine, education, theater, or music are acknowledged by peers or the world in general. People finding favor with people isn't unusual.

Have you ever thought about how rich it would be to have God find favor with you? I'm awed to think of our holy God finding favor with us human beings, but He does.

Noah lived in a sin-filled world much like ours today. (Human beings haven't changed much over the centuries—we just call "sin" something else.) Yet despite the wickedness around him, Noah lived a life that was pleasing to God. It's important to realize that Noah didn't find favor with God because of his individual goodness but because of his faith in Him. You and I are judged by that same standard. Are we faithful and obedient to God?

Although Noah was upright and blameless before God, he wasn't perfect. Genuine faith isn't always perfect faith. But despite his human failings, Noah walked with God (Genesis 6:9). The circumstances of his life could have blocked his fellowship with God, but his heart attitude enabled him to find favor with Him.

Are you seeking favor from God or honor from the world? Noah wanted only to please God. When you go to God and admit you're a sinner, you're pleasing Him. At that time, you'll experience God's grace and move into a closer relationship with Jesus Christ.

May you, like Noah, find favor in God's sight and be honored by Him.

Today's Action

Do something to find favor with God. And do it under grace, not under law.

Prayer

Father God, help me be faithful and obedient so I might find favor with You. Amen.

NEVER FORSAKEN

The LORD knows the days of the blameless,
and their inheritance will be forever.

PSALM 37:18

I don't know if you're like me, but when I look at what's happening in the world, I see very little hope for the future. I'm concerned for my children and grandchildren—and for my great-grandchildren.

But then the Lord brings before me Psalm 37. In this passage, David exhorts the righteous to trust in the Lord. Even when it looks like evil will overpower righteousness, God never abandons His children (verse 25). Though they may experience the heartaches of a sinful, fallen world, God's children are never forsaken. In fact, His blessings will extend to the next generation (verse 26).

During my quiet time with the Lord in this particular psalm, certain key phrases comfort me:

- Do not fret; be not envious (verse 1).
- Trust in the Lord; cultivate faithfulness (verse 3).
- Delight yourself in the Lord; He will give you abundantly the desires of your heart (verse 4).
- Commit your way to the Lord; trust also in Him (verse 5).
- Rest in the Lord; wait patiently (verse 7).
- Cease from anger; do not fret (verse 8).
- The humble will inherit the land (verse 11).

- Depart from evil (verse 27).
- Wait for the Lord (verse 34).

Then in verses 39 and 40, we read of the great blessings we receive as children of God: "The salvation of the righteous is from the LORD; He is [our] strength in time of trouble. And the LORD helps [us], and delivers [us]; He delivers [us] from the wicked and saves [us], because [we] take refuge in Him."

As I leave my time of prayer, I'm again able to face the negative issues of the day. Why? Because centuries ago, David took time to write this poetic psalm of comfort to remind us that the Lord will never forsake us.

Today's Action
Read and meditate on Psalm 37. Start learning to trust, delight, commit, rest, be humble, and wait.

Prayer
Father God, give me assurance that righteousness still deflects evil, as it did centuries ago. Amen.

In the Lord's Tent

O Lord, who may abide in Your tent?
Who may dwell on Your holy hill?

Psalm 15:1

In Psalm 15:1-5, David describes the character of the person who qualifies to be a guest in God's tent. The parallel questions of verse 1 are answered in the following four verses by an elevenfold description of the righteous person who's upright in deed, word, attitude, and finances. These qualities, which aren't natural, are imparted to us by God and His Holy Spirit.

Let's see what this great psalm tells us about the man who may dwell in the Lord's tent:

1. He walks blamelessly (verse 2).
2. He does what is righteous (verse 2).
3. He speaks the truth from his heart (verse 2).
4. He has no slander on his tongue (verse 3).
5. He does his neighbor no harm (verse 3).
6. He casts no slur on his friends (verse 3).
7. He despises an evil man (verse 4).
8. He honors those who fear the Lord (verse 4).
9. He keeps his oath even when it hurts (verse 4).
10. He lends his money without interest (verse 5).
11. He doesn't accept a bribe (verse 5).

These are honorable characteristics! We certainly can appreciate the virtue of this type of man. But many times we look on the life of a righteous person and say to ourselves, *It must be easy for him to be a Christian. He evidently doesn't struggle with sin like I do!* Yet all people trying to live a righteous life must choose to serve the Lord. It isn't easy for any of us. We must decide to do what's right moment by moment.

David closed this psalm by stating, "He who does these things will never be shaken" (verse 5). What a great promise! Live it with great faith, and dwell in the Lord's tent.

Today's Action

Inventory your level of character and see what areas you need to work on. Write down three to five things you could do to improve them.

Prayer

Father God, today I willfully decide to believe and live the Scriptures of old, precept by precept and line by line. Amen.

I Love You

Jesus said, "Simon son of John, do you love me?"
He answered, "Yes, Lord, you know that I love you."
Jesus said, "Take care of my sheep."
JOHN 21:16 NIV

Many of us go through life wondering if our family and friends really love us. We feel insecure about how they feel about us because we're not always sure where we stand with them. And even though we can tell—and show—the people in our lives that we love them, they don't always seem to catch what we're saying because they're reaching out to test our love.

Jesus isn't insecure in the least, but in John 21, three times He asks Peter whether he really loves Him (verses 15-17). I believe these basic questions correspond to Peter's three denials of Jesus (John 13:38). In all of His love, Jesus wanted to give Peter a second chance to follow Him. He didn't want Peter to go through life with the stigma of denying Jesus hanging over his head. He wanted Peter to know he was forgiven for his wrongdoing, and that he could have a valuable ministry in spreading the gospel throughout the world.

Then Jesus let Peter know that the decision to follow Him—and to feed His people—would cost him something (John 21:18-19). There would be a price—even death. But when Jesus said, "Follow me," Peter did.

Yes, love has its price. It can cost us time, energy, commitment, money, devotion—or all five. Selfish people take without giving back, but a true lover of people is always giving and giving and giving.

Is anyone in your life asking this very question: "Do you love me?" What's your reply?

Today's Action

Let your family and friends know you love them, and look them straight in the eyes when you give them this important message.

Prayer

Father God, let my words and actions show those around me that I love them. Amen.

The Faithful Guide

That they should seek God,
if perhaps they might grope for Him and find Him,
though He is not far from each one of us.

Acts 17:27

Each of us has a unique story about how we found God, but none are as unique as General Naaman's story found in 2 Kings 5:1-16. The general had taken captive a slave girl from Israel, and she waited on his wife. This young maiden was concerned about the general's leprosy. She told her mistress that Naaman should find the prophet of God in Israel—Elisha. She knew if he found the prophet, he would also find her God.

We never hear more about this faithful slave girl, but we know Naaman found Elisha and—finally—did as he commanded. He bathed seven times in the Jordan River, was healed from his disease, and believed the miracle was from the true God. This all happened because a young slave girl was so concerned about his well-being that she directed him to where he could meet the real God.

Never far away, God wants all of us to find Him. And He often uses ordinary people to lead the way. Then when we come to Jesus, we're healed and made whole. This is encouragement for you to take your heavy burdens, sins, and illnesses to Him, expecting a miracle. Jesus is never far away from those who are faithful to Him.

Today's Action

Point someone to God by sharing your faith with them.

Prayer

Father God, thank You for sending Jesus to wash away my sins with His blood. Help me always be His faithful servant. Amen.

The Purpose of Life

*I press on toward the goal
for the prize of the upward
call of God in Christ Jesus.*

Philippians 3:14

Struggling to understand the death of his loved one, a man courageously said, "I still don't see the purpose, but I don't give up. Somehow I feel that in my very struggle, I'm choosing to say there is meaning and purpose."

As Christians, our lives have purpose. We weren't planted on this earth just for a certain length of time; there's more to living than being alive. In John 10:10, Jesus states that He came so we might have abundant life. We should live life to the fullest, then, and we should reflect Christ with our lifestyle.

When we understand life, we'll no longer struggle with death. A great promise regarding this principle is found in John 11:25-26, when Jesus said to Martha, "I am the resurrection and the life; he who believes in Me shall live even if he dies, and everyone who lives and believes in Me shall never die."

Do you believe this? How much you believe and live this promise determines how you will face not just death but life. Know that your life here on this earth has purpose—and live out that purpose with God's help.

Today's Action

Write out a "life statement of purpose." Then share this statement with those you're close to.

Prayer

Father God, I know You came to give me life abundantly, and I want to live a life that reflects Your love to those around me.

Amen.

Precious Treasure

We have this treasure in earthen vessels,
that the surpassing greatness of the power
may be of God and not from ourselves.
2 Corinthians 4:7

In today's Scripture, we read that we are earthen vessels—jars of clay—and that we hold the great treasure of the gospel within. Simply stated, Christianity is Jesus Christ, the treasure, residing in the Christian, a clay pot. And God trusts us—even commands us—to share that treasure with other people. Isn't it interesting that you and I hide our treasures in vaults and safe deposit boxes, but God trusts His treasure to a common clay pot? The only value our clay pot has is due to the treasure inside.

Do you honestly believe God can use you to do the work He's called you to do for His kingdom? If we believed and acted on this promise, God's kingdom would reign more fully in our hearts, our homes, our churches, our cities, our country, and our world. Value your precious treasure—and then share it with others.

Today's Action

Meditate on this question: In what parts of your life do you think God wants to use you for His kingdom?

Prayer

Father God, don't let me hide my treasure in an earthen vessel.
I want others around me to see what a precious treasure I have.
Amen.

The Privilege of Close Fellowship

That Christ may dwell in your hearts through faith.

Ephesians 3:17

A man was giving his testimony of salvation at an open air meeting. God had miraculously changed him from a drunkard into a devoted Christian, and now he radiated the presence of Christ. As he spoke, someone in the crowd called out, "You talk as if Jesus Christ lived next door to you!"

"No," answered the man. "He lives nearer than that. He dwells in my heart!"

Someone once observed that Christianity is not a religion but a relationship. Yes, this relationship with our Savior is much closer than our family ties. Through the presence of the Holy Spirit, Jesus lives in every believer. Many religions of the world find it difficult to accept the idea of a God who says He will dwell in our hearts. For instance, in the Jewish faith, one doesn't talk to God in such a personal way.

As Christians, we can have close fellowship with Christ daily. His maximum assurance is that someday we will spend eternity with Him in heaven. We have the blessing of a friendship with God, and He dwells in our hearts through faith.

Today's Action

If He doesn't already, ask God to dwell in your heart. And if He does, thank Him for being such a caring, approachable God.

Prayer

Father God, may my heart be Your dwelling place, and let me clearly hear Your directions for my life. Amen.

Exiled

Build houses and live in them;
and plant gardens and eat their produce.
JEREMIAH 29:5

When the prophet Jeremiah sent a letter to the Jews who'd been exiled to Babylon, he exhorted them to live as normal a life as possible as they continued to wait for God's deliverance.

Maybe you've found yourself in exile—in a place you don't want to be, with people you don't want to be with, doing things you don't want to do. This type of situation requires you to daily decide how to react. Will you be a victim and lament, "Woe is me—I'm just not going to do anything"? Or will your reply be that of a victor, as Jeremiah's letter suggested: "Build houses and live in them; and plant gardens, and eat their produce"?

We find two groups of people in the world today: victims and victors. Almost every social, political, and economic question boils down to how people react when they find themselves in one group or the other. But we need to do the very best with today's situation, whatever that might be. God is here with us, and we need to make it work.

We all have times when we find ourselves in a different place as if in exile. How will we respond to a new job, new friends, a new school, or a new church? Exile reveals what really matters and permits us to again strive to do what's important in life.

Today's Action

Decide to be a victor when in a time of exile.

Prayer

Father God, this time of exile is helping me depend on You more each day. Thank You that You're always with me, even when I feel alone. Amen.

TEMPTATION REVEALED

Do not enter the path of the wicked
and do not proceed in the way of evil men.
Avoid it, do not pass by it; turn away from it and pass on.

PROVERBS 4:14-15

Several artists were asked to illustrate their concepts of temptation. When their paintings were unveiled, some of them had depicted mankind's attempt to achieve fame and fortune at any cost, and others had pictured mankind's struggle against the alluring desires of the flesh.

The prize-winning canvas, however, portrayed a pastoral scene in which a man was walking along a quiet country lane among inviting shade trees and lovely wildflowers. In the distance, the way divided into two roads—one leading to the right, the other to the left. The artist was seeking to convey the idea that sin's allurements are extremely subtle at first—just an innocent-looking fork in the road!

We continually struggle with temptation, the ugly hands of sin reaching out to grasp away from us any goodness we have. Few of us would go straight from point A to point B, but we'll make smaller and easier choices toward evil before finally giving in to temptation.

When we face temptation, we must be aware of and sensitive to taking that first compromising step.

Today's Action

Decide to keep to the right when you come to a fork in the road.

Prayer

Father God, give me clear discernment when I come to a fork in the road. Help me turn toward Your righteousness. Amen.

PLANNED NEGLECT

Daniel...continued kneeling on his knees three times a day, praying and giving thanks before his God, as he had been doing previously.

DANIEL 6:10

In her book *A Practical Guide to Prayer*, Dorothy Haskin told about a noted concert violinist who was asked the secret to her mastery of the instrument. The woman answered the question with two words: "Planned neglect." Then she explained:

> There were many things that used to demand my time. When I went to my room after breakfast, I made my bed, straightened the room, dusted, and did whatever seemed necessary. When I finished my work, I turned to my violin practice. That system prevented me from accomplishing what I should on the violin. So I reversed things. I deliberately planned to neglect everything else until my practice period was complete. And that program of planned neglect is the secret of my success.[17]

What priority does your quiet time with the Lord have? Do you just try to fit it in sometime during the day, or do you systematically give God top priority? We have to plan our neglect of other things in order to preserve our prayer time. Unless we discipline ourselves and make a deliberate effort, little things will keep us from establishing a consistent devotional life.

One of my favorite mottos is this: Say no to good things to save yes for the best. If we give God our squeezed-in or leftover part of our schedules, our quiet time won't be effective for growth.

Today's Action

Start your practice of "planned neglect"—and give attention to what truly matters.

Prayer

Father God, give me the discipline to say no to good things so I can give first priority to You. Amen.

Knowing God's Will

*All Scripture is breathed out by God and profitable for teaching,
for reproof, for correction, for training in righteousness.*
2 Timothy 3:16

How do we know God's will? Through the pages of His Word, the Bible. This is why it's important to read the Word of God every day. It's where we learn God's principles and directions for life and why we can be certain of the gospel.

The Bible itself tells us:

- I am not ashamed of the gospel, for it is the power of God for salvation to everyone who believes (Romans 1:16).
- Blessed is he who reads and those who hear the words of the prophecy, and heed the things which are written in it, for the time is near (Revelation 1:3).
- The unfolding of Thy words gives light; it gives understanding to the simple (Psalm 119:130).
- All Scripture is breathed out by God and profitable for teaching, for reproof, for correction, and for training in righteousness, that the man of God may be complete, equipped for every good work (2 Timothy 3:16-17).

If you want to discover God's will, you must devote yourself to spending time in His Word and asking Him for understanding and guidance.

Today's Action

Write down two decisions you need to make, and then ask God for His guidance.

Prayer

Father God, give me a discerning spirit when it comes to knowing Your plan for my life. Amen.

THE POWER OF SILENCE

Jesus made no further answer;
so Pilate was amazed.

MARK 15:5

Oh, if only I had remained silent more often. But I didn't. Through time, however, I've learned that silence is one of the greatest virtues of the Christian lifestyle.

Commenting on the silences of Jesus, British writer Jessie Penn-Lewis said the Christian who's living close to the Lord will manifest humility and self-control under the most trying circumstances. She wrote:

> We will be silent in our lowly service among others, not seeking to be "seen of men." Silent while we stoop to serve the very ones who betrayed us. Silent when forced by others to some position where apparent rivalry with another much-abused servant of God seems imminent, only to be hushed by utter self-effacement in our silent withdrawal without explanation, irrespective of our "rights."[18]

In our assertive generation, we seem to insist on our rights, and we argue to make people understand our position. But if we find ourselves having to verbally defend our actions, then we may need to learn more from the silence of Jesus.

Today's Action

If you find yourself wanting to answer back in a conflict or disagreement today, try keeping silent instead.

Prayer

Father God, thank You for this reminder to keep silent, because I often want to set the record straight. Amen.

Working for God

Whatever you do, do your work heartily,
as for the Lord rather than for men.
Colossians 3:23

Does your work seem like a waste of time? If it does, try changing your mindset. Consider your place of work a place of ministry, and then perform your duties as if you're doing them for Jesus. He's the one you're really serving.

Why do I do what I do? Is it to please man or God? These are two questions we must ask ourselves, because how we answer reveals how we look at life. If we work to please people, we'll never be satisfied, because people will always expect more from us. If we work to please God, however, then we'll hop out of bed each morning, eager to see what the new day brings.

If God's purposes are to be fulfilled, we must not neglect the ordinary tasks in our pursuit of the glorious ones. Meals must be cooked, trash must be collected, assembly lines must be manned, and children must be tended. Every service done unto God is significant, and we'll be fulfilled in our work when we do it for Him.

Today's Action

Whatever God gives you to do today, do it for Him.

Prayer

Father God, help me think of my job as a ministry.
May others always see Christ reflected in my work
and in my attitude. Amen.

ORDINARY PEOPLE

Who has despised the day of small things?
ZECHARIAH 4:10

We live in an age of comparison, looking at people's homes, cars, and other possessions to judge if ours are better or nicer. And the world says we have to have the biggest, because small isn't good enough. But if we buy into this line of thought, we'll spend our whole lives thinking we must work longer, smarter, and harder to improve our status in life.

When a small boy donated his two fishes and bread to Jesus, the Lord blessed his tiny lunch, and it became a meal for thousands of hungry people. There was even food to spare (John 6:9-14). Likewise, we must depend on God's ability to take our smallness and use it for His glory.

One of my favorite songs is "Ordinary People," which reflects on how God uses regular people to do His work. The Christian hall of fame is truly made up of men and women who were willing to serve the Lord in any way possible. Little is much if God is in it.

Today's Action

Step forward and volunteer for something that might seem small to the world.

Prayer

Father God, I ask that I not despise small jobs,
because I realize that You are a God who will
abundantly bless those things that seem
insignificant to the world. Amen.

An Outcast's Love

A certain Samaritan, who was on a journey,
came upon him; and when he saw him,
he felt compassion.

LUKE 10:33

The Samaritans were descendants of colonists the Assyrian kings planted in Palestine after the fall of the Northern Kingdom in 721 BC. The Jews despised them because of their mixed Gentile and Jewish blood and their worship, which centered on Mount Gerizim. On this mountain, the Samaritans had built a temple to rival the one in Jerusalem, from which they had long been separated politically and religiously.

In the parable from Jesus found in Luke 10:30-37, two travelers passed by an injured man—even the priest. But then a man regarded as alien and foreign—a Samaritan—bandaged the victim's wounds, took him to an inn, fed him, and rented a room for him to stay in until he recovered.

This certainly reflects genuine love, for the Samaritan in the story didn't even know the injured man. Maybe this outcast understood the pain of neglect and rejection, and that's why he ministered to this man in need with such compassion.

Let us follow his example and show every person we happen upon our love.

Today's Action

Perform a "good Samaritan" act with genuine care despite any cost.

Prayer

Father God, I need to be more compassionate to those in need.
Help me do a better job of noticing the needs of others
and caring for them. Amen.

The Greatest Motive

Walk in a manner worthy of the Lord,
to please Him in all respects.
Colossians 1:10

A first grader beamed with satisfaction as he handed his parents a spelling test on which his teacher had written "100—Good Work!" The boy later said, "I showed this to Dad and Mom because I knew it would please them." I can just see him riding home on the bus, hardly able to wait for the moment when his parents would express their excitement over how well he'd done.

A strong desire to please God is the highest incentive we have for doing His will. We may have other worthy motives, such as the inner satisfaction gained from doing what's right or the anticipation of receiving rewards in heaven. But we bring the greatest glory to God when we obey and serve Him because we long to do what brings Him delight.

Many times Jesus put His own desires aside and chose to please His Father. He prayed, "Not My will, but Thine be done" (Luke 22:42 kjv). His greatest motive was His desire to please God. That's quite an incentive for us too.

Today's Action

Do something to honor God.

Prayer

Father God, may I be a God-pleaser more than a people-pleaser.
Amen.

The Pursuit of Godliness

With a long life I will satisfy him,
and let him behold My salvation.

PSALM 91:16

In America, it seems as though we're constantly going through major changes with our health insurance options. Healthcare is a major political issue. How will we take care of the sick, and who will pay for these services?

The Bible often associates longevity with godliness. And in Psalm 91, the Lord not only declares that He will deliver, protect, and honor the one who trusts in Him, but give them a long life, showing them His salvation.

But in the medical profession, it's well known that a sizable percentage of human disease and suffering on this earth is directly traceable to worry, fear, conflict, immorality, and dissipation—unwholesome thinking and unclean living. It follows, then, that if people pursued godly lives, much of the illness we find in America and throughout the world would be wiped out, leading to the long life God wants us to have.

Godliness does lead to blessings—even during dark times, even when illness befalls us. And if we place our trust in God and pursue Him, we can look for His favor in our lives, including His gift of eternal salvation.

Today's Action
Identify how you can better trust and pursue the Lord today.

Prayer
Father God, even during dark times, I thank You for Your abundant promises. And I look forward to the life you have for me, as long as it may be here on earth and throughout eternity.
Amen.

THE PURPOSE OF SUFFERING

After you have suffered for a little while,
the God of all grace,
who called you to His eternal glory in Christ,
will Himself perfect, confirm, strengthen
and establish you.

1 PETER 5:10

Wouldn't it be wonderful to grow into full Christian maturity without suffering? But I've talked to many godly senior citizens—both men and women—and I'm amazed at the challenging events that have made them such dedicated people of God.

These friends have shared the pain that helped mold them into Christlike beings. Oh, yes, they've had their times of exuberance, but they didn't seem to build the inner character Peter talks about in today's verse. Peter wanted to give a message of encouragement to those Christians scattered throughout the Roman Empire, because he knew a lot of suffering would be inflicted by the then pagan society. He said not to count the hard times as loss, but to rejoice, because after a while God Himself would perfect (make them mature), confirm, strengthen, and establish them. These are the attributes of my senior citizen friends.

When you're suffering, know that God is molding you, helping you become more like Christ. So count it all joy.

Today's Action

Meditate on how God is using today's circumstances to help you mature in your walk with Jesus.

Prayer

Father God, I look forward to the good work You'll do in my life. Mold me and shape me as You will. Amen.

Winning the Race

Let endurance have its perfect result,
so that you may be perfect and complete, lacking in nothing.

James 1:4

A few years ago my family visited Lake Tahoe to ski during the Christmas break. As I walked on the icy slopes of this beautiful area, my eyes were full of the best—the best cars, the best skis, the best clothes, and the best beauty. I couldn't believe my eyes. I'd never seen so much sizzle in one place. I said to myself, *No way can I compete with this.* But then after being coaxed into a group ski lesson that included members of the sizzle group, I found they couldn't ski any better than I could!

Today's Scripture teaches that perseverance is enduring with patience. In the Bible, perseverance describes Christians who faithfully endure and remain steadfast in the face of opposition, attack, and discouragement. When we persevere with patience, we exhibit our ability to endure with calmness and without complaint. As believers, we must daily commit ourselves to godly living.

The world tells us everything should feel good, and *commitment* and *discipline* aren't words it's comfortable with. But perseverance doesn't always feel good. It sometimes demands denial of self and presents us with pain. That's why trusting in God and having faith in His guidance is so important.

Scripture is clear when it teaches we are to persevere:

- in prayer (Ephesians 6:18)
- in obedience (Revelation 14:12)
- in self-control (2 Peter 1:5-7)

And Scripture promises us these blessings if we endure:

- final deliverance (Matthew 24:13)
- rewarded faith (Hebrews 11:6)
- eternal inheritance (Revelation 21:7)

Today's Action

Jot down any struggles you're having. Then beside each one, list what you think God is trying to teach you through them.

Prayer

Father God, help me see what You're trying to teach me amid life's difficulties. Amen.

Jonathan and David

The soul of Jonathan was knit to the soul of David,
and Jonathan loved him as himself.

1 Samuel 18:1

English writer Samuel Johnson wrote, "We cannot tell the precise moment when friendship is formed. As in filling a vessel drop by drop, there is at last a drop which makes it run over; so in a series of kindness there is at last one which makes the heart run over."[19]

In 1 Samuel 18, 19, and 23, we discover one of the finest examples of friendship—the deep relationship between Jonathan, the king's son, and David, a shepherd boy. They accepted each other even though they were far apart socially. They depended on each other's strengths to shore up their individual weaknesses, and they exhibited several traits found in healthy friendships:

- unconditional love
- personal enjoyment
- mutual acceptance
- mutual interests
- mutual commitment
- mutual loyalty

To be a friend, you must be involved in the other person's life—solid and lasting friendship takes time and commitment.

You have to be willing to put your friend's needs above your own. But once you do this, you'll have a friend for life.

Today's Action

Take inventory of who your real friends are. Then give them each a call and let them know they're important to you.

Prayer

Father God, thank You for my friends who love me, and help me show my love for them. Amen.

Where Is Your Joy?

*These things I have spoken to you
so that My joy may be in you, and that
your joy may be made full.*
John 15:11

Sometimes after we meet someone in church, we walk away thinking, *Where is their joy? If they once had it, they've certainly lost it.* In today's verse, we see that Jesus has given us abundant joy. He gave us a fullness of joy—and that's a lot. Do members of your family consider you a joyful person? If you asked them this question, what would they say? I encourage you to ask them.

I remember one of my Sunday school teachers writing this on the chalkboard:

Jesus 0 You

The zero illustrates that there's nothing between Jesus and you—and that's the gospel truth. In order to have joy, all we need is Jesus and ourselves—nothing more, nothing less.

Today's Action

Read these verses to help you find more joy in your life: Psalm 104:34, Luke 10:20, and Acts 2:28.

Prayer

*Father God, thank You
for Your radiance. Life would
be gloomy without Your influence
on my life. Amen.*

Choosing Silence

Be still, and know that I am God.

Psalm 46:10 niv

Have you ever stepped outside on a cold, snowy morning before the animals and birds have put their tracks in the freshly fallen snow? What an exuberance that creates in the heart. It's so very quiet, with not a sound echoed. This is what I envision stillness to be—such a contrast to the noise of freeway, airport, and other sounds that bombarded us—the blare of the radio, the TV, the children, the arguments.

Habakkuk 2:20 tells us, "The Lord is in His holy temple. Let all the earth be silent before Him." Experiencing this silence isn't a choice; it's more like a command. If we aren't silent by our own choosing, there will be a time when and a place where our physical bodies give out because of all the stimulation. We'll lie sleepless because of illness, heartache, grief, or anxiety.

In those moments of quietness, we can learn lessons we chose not to learn on our own. Don't wait until the silence is cast upon you. Choose to practice daily stillness and silence.

Today's Action
Set aside some time to be silent before God.

Prayer
*Father God, I'm committed
to developing a daily time of quietness—
just You and me. Amen.*

Red Lights Mean Stop!

Oh that my ways may be established to keep Thy statutes!
Psalm 119:5

Psalm 119 conveys the truth that the Word of God contains everything man needs to know. If you live in a mid-to-large city, you know the trick of trying to hit all the green lights on your most traveled route. If you're successful with this, you might yell with exuberance, "I did it—I didn't have to stop once!" When the occasional miscalculation occurs, however, and you come to one of those big, yellow lights, you have a decision to make: Will you risk going through, or will you stop?

Most of us don't like red lights in our lives, but they serve a valuable purpose. In traffic they prevent accidents; in life God puts them there as prohibitions against selfishness, envy, hatred, lust, pride, and irreverence. When these personal red lights flash on, we need to stop immediately. If we run the lights, we're really heading for trouble.

Be as respectful of God's red lights as you are of city statutes. Remember, red lights mean stop, and their presence in life often means the Lord is trying to teach you something.

Today's Action

Ask yourself if you're ready to stop at God's red lights.

Prayer

Father God, help me anticipate and recognize
any red lights ahead of me, and prepare me
to stop at them and listen to what
You have to teach me. Amen.

CREATOR OR CREATED?

Thus says the LORD…
"I am the first and I am the last,
and there is no God besides Me."

ISAIAH 44:6

As men, we struggle with who will be our god. Will it be a person, a job, wealth, a possession, or the one true, almighty God? Idolatry is placing our longings for what only God can provide in the hands of a created creature instead of the Creator's. When we base our lives on false gods created by man instead of depending on God the Creator, we eventually realize that life doesn't have meaning and is void of fulfillment.

The writers of Scripture are quite clear that dependency on a false god will result in loss, pain, and shame (Isaiah 42:17; 44:9-11). A false god will leave emptiness and disappointment.

We need to continually evaluate our lives to see why we do what we do. What is our motivation? Are we trying to please the Creator, or the created? If we're honest with ourselves, we can change course and go in another direction. It's important that we let God work in our lives. We need to be as soft as new clay so we can be remolded. If we become hard, we're brittle and fragile.

We need to keep our eyes on the Lord so He can direct our paths.

Today's Action

Look in the mirror. Who do you see? The Creator or the created?

Prayer

Father God, restore my vision so I see only You. Amen.

How Can We Give Thanks?

In everything give thanks; for this is God's will for you in Christ Jesus.
1 Thessalonians 5:18

First Thessalonians 5:18 is one of the most challenging Scriptures to understand. How do we say "Thank You, God" for hard situations and bad events? I struggled with this question until I realized this verse says *in* everything, not *for* everything.

The expression "in everything" is not the same as "for everything." We don't give thanks for evil or for evil results. But we *can* give thanks when we're in those situations, because we know God is working. We can remain grateful even when our lives are touched by evil, because we live in Christ Jesus. We're living eternally, not temporally. God gives us special attention and care because we're one of His children. He's continually transforming us into the image of Jesus, and that's where our thanks comes in.

The well-known Bible commentator Matthew Henry made the following entry in his diary after he'd been robbed: "Let me be thankful first because I was never robbed before; second, although they took my [possessions], they did not take my life; third, because although they took my all, it was not much; and fourth, because it was I who was robbed, not I who robbed."[20]

Remember to give thanks in all situations—and to trust that God will see you through.

Today's Action

In everything today, give thanks.

Prayer

Father God, I pray that Your will be done in my life. Help me give thanks in all circumstances. Amen.

MELTING YOUR ENEMY'S HEART

I say to you, love your enemies,
and pray for those who persecute you.
MATTHEW 5:44

Love my enemies? Are you kidding? Why would I want to do that? I'm so enjoying hating them."

Have you ever felt like that? I have. But in Matthew 5, Jesus gives three reasons to love those who persecute us:

- When we show them kindness, we're imitating our heavenly Father, who makes His sun rise on the evil and on the good, and sends rain on the just and the unjust (verse 45).
- We're to love our foes, because there's no reward for loving only those who love us (verse 46).
- Gracious treatment of our enemies sets us apart from the ungodly. Jesus said, "If you greet your brothers only, what do you do more than others?" (verse 47).

The best way to defeat Satan in this area is to make a friend out of an enemy. This act doesn't come naturally, and we're able to do it only with the strength the Holy Spirit provides. When you melt your enemy's heart, you open up the possibility of becoming friends with them—and the possibility for both of you to grow closer to God.

Today's Action

Pray for an enemy who persecutes you, and then let your prayer go before you.

Prayer

Father God, give my heart the warmth of love so that I can melt an enemy's heart with Your love. Amen.

The Making of a Home

Unless the LORD builds the house,
they labor in vain who build it.

PSALM 127:1

As a young dad, I sometimes wondered if we actually had a home or merely a stopover place to eat, do laundry, hang around, and sleep. Was it just a place to repair broken objects, mow the lawn, pay off the mortgage, paint, wallpaper, and install new carpet and furniture?

I finally figured out that a real home is much more than all that. It's a place where, together, people live, grow, laugh, learn, and create. A home should also be a place to cry and even die—a trauma center for the whole family.

We don't have to be perfect—just forgiven. Everywhere else—school, work, neighborhood, church—people expect us to be perfect. But our home is a place where we can be ourselves. We all need a place to be just us, with no pretense. We can laugh when we feel like it and cry when we need to. We can grow, we can make mistakes, we can agree, and we can disagree. Home should be a place where happy experiences occur—a place sheltered from the problems of the world and a place of love, acceptance, and security.

As husbands and dads, what can we do to have a home like God intended? When something is broken, we go back to the instruction manual, and in this case that's the Bible. The home is God's idea—not something invented by twenty-first-century Americans.

In the original plan of creation, God designed the home to be the foundation of society—a place to meet the mental, spiritual, physical, and emotional needs of people.

The home is God's loving shelter for growing to maturity. We need to return to the words of today's Scripture verse: "Unless the Lord builds the house, they labor in vain who build it." Not only is God the designer, but He also wants to take the headship of family life. He wants to guide and give love, peace, and forgiveness abundantly.

Solomon spoke to this subject in Proverbs 24:3–4: "By wisdom a house is built, and through understanding it is established; through knowledge its rooms are filled with rare and beautiful treasures" (NIV). We've got our work cut out for us if we want to create a true home. We must live life with a big purpose—to make not just a house but a home.

Today's Action

Pray for your home and its members.

Prayer

Father God, You know I want my house to be more than just a place. I want it to be a home, and to that end, I yield to Your leadership. Give me wisdom, understanding, and knowledge. Amen.

God Keeps His Promises

The LORD is trustworthy in all he promises.

PSALM 145:13 NIV

God always keeps His promises because His character will not let Him fall back. And He finds joy in keeping His promises.

We live in a day when all aspects of life are undermined by dishonesty. For example, couples have lost most of their retirement funds because they believed executives' promises made with their fingers crossed behind their backs. We look to our sports heroes, our political leaders, our corporate leadership, the stars of movies and television, and even our spiritual leaders hoping they'll show us how people of character live. But each time we feel comfortable that a certain personality has the answer, we're disappointed by some revelation of broken promises. Oh, how desperate our world is for people of character!

We expect people to do what they say they're going to do, and we patiently wait, and nothing happens. We're disappointed when a plumber, an electrician, a painter, or a coworker doesn't do what they promised. They miss the appointment or don't deliver their product on time. Even parents tell their children that such-and-such will happen on Saturday, but then it doesn't happen as promised. How many children go to their rooms to cry because a promise was broken?

We're so fortunate to have Someone who never goes back on His promises. God the Father, Jesus the Son, and the Holy Spirit always keep their word. If they said it, you can believe it. Let's all learn from the masters of character.

Today's Action

Make and keep a promise to someone today—even a small one. Make this practice a discipline of your faith.

Prayer

Father God, thanks for being a promise-keeper. You are the model for every man who wants to be honorable. You give great confidence from Your Word because I know You won't break Your promise. If You said it, I believe it. Amen.

Be Careful What You Say

Death and life are in the power of the tongue,
and those who love it will eat its fruit.

Proverbs 18:21

The tongue is a powerful tool—it can bring us death, or it can bring us life. James gives a strong warning about this power: "Everyone must be quick to hear, slow to speak and slow to anger; for the anger of man does not achieve the righteousness of God" (James 1:19–20). Whether words give us death or life depends on how we choose them.

We communicate in so many different ways, and often our looks and touches communicate as strongly as our words. These nonverbal signals transmit our feelings in a strong fashion, but words are most often used for communication. We desperately need to tell others what we're thinking, how we're feeling, what we're dealing with, and what our dreams are.

How we put our thoughts into words will make a difference in whether our relationships are strong or weak, full of excitement or agony and pain, full of wellness or destruction. A key verse that guides us in this area is Ephesians 4:29: "Let no unwholesome word proceed from your mouth, but only such a word as is good for edification according to the need of the moment, so that it will give grace to those who hear."

Communication is so very important to healthy relationships. Therefore, we need to learn as much as possible about how to develop this skill. Listening is as valuable as speaking. If we're to have open communication, we must be vulnerable and honest, but we must also be good listeners. Don't be the kind of person who waits for a break in someone else's words so you can jump in and give your opinion. When we're good listeners, we allow the other person the freedom to share without fear, rejection, or negative judgment. Good listening creates good bonding, and the better we bond, the closer we become.

When individuals are able to resolve their differences in a healthy fashion, it permits them to disagree in the same healthy way in the future. And by being careful what you say and listening, you let others know they're important to you.

Today's Action

As you go about your day, pay attention to how well you're quick to hear, slow to speak, and slow to anger.

Prayer

Father God, give me the desire to be a good communicator. Let me listen before I speak, and let my tongue be quiet until I know all the facts. Then let me be careful with my words. Amen.

What Would Jesus Do?

You have been called for this purpose, since Christ also suffered for you, leaving you an example for you to follow in His steps.

1 Peter 2:21

Many years ago I read Charles M. Sheldon's book *In His Steps*, the story of a man who made a conscious effort to walk in the steps of Jesus. Before saying anything, doing anything, going anywhere, or making any decisions, he asked himself what Jesus would do and tried to do the same. Although living like Jesus was nearly impossible, this experience changed the man's life forever.

During our time on earth, daily situations will reveal our character. But will our character point others toward Jesus? We do well to look to Jesus and His example of a godly life. He showed us how to live with kindness, gentleness, empathy, and affection. He was always loving, forgiving, merciful, and patient. He had a sense of justice and compassion for the suffering and persecuted, and He willingly took a stand for what was right in God's eyes.

Jesus also tells us that He knows our pains, our grief, and the tragedy of friends betraying us. He knows how hard it is to live in a world full of sickness and sin we can do very little about. But what we can do—and this is following in Jesus' footsteps—is bring people to the One who forgives, heals, and helps. We can also let God work in our own hearts and lives so He can make us more Christlike—and that's certainly something the world needs today.

No, we can't be exactly like Jesus. Our humanness and sin get in the way. But we can develop a teachable spirit. We can love God with all our heart, soul, mind, and strength. We can let Him transform us into more selfless, joyful people so that our character will reveal the likeness of Jesus.

As Jesus' representatives in the world today, we walk in His steps when we help the helpless, pray for the sick, feed and clothe the homeless, and support those whom God lifts up to minister in places we can't go.

Today's Action

Walk in Jesus' steps today by doing something Christlike.

Prayer

Father God, grant me a new revelation, and help me step out and trust You in a new way. Amen.

NOTES

1. "What Governs Life," J. Wilbur Chapman quote, Bible.org, https://www
   .bing.com/search?q=What+Governs+Life+%7C+Bible.org&cvid=e88bf42
   263fd49bc99defa9f9302e85d&gs_lcrp=EgZjaHJvbWUyBggAEEUYOTIEC
   AEQADIECAIQADIECAMQADIECAQQADIECAUQADIECAYQADIE
   CAcQADIECAgQANIBCDExNjJqMGo5qAIAsAIA&FORM=ANAB01&
   PC=HCTS.

2. William R. Alger quote, BrainyQuotes, https://www.brainyquote.com/
   authors/william-r-alger-quotes.

3. Martin Luther quote, BrainyQuotes, https://www.brainyquote.com/topics/
   hands-quotes#:~:text=I%20have%20held%20many%20things%20in%20
   my%20hands%2C,his%20brain%20and%20his%20heart%20is%20an%20
   artist.

4. "Rest Only in God," Bible Hub, quoting from The Biblical Illustrator, Electronic Database. Copyright © 2002, 2003, 2006, 2011 by BibleSoft, Inc. All
   rights reserved. Used by permission. BibleSoft.com, https://biblehub.com/
   sermons/pub/rest_only_in_god.htm.

5. *If You Ask Me: Essential Advice from Eleanor Roosevelt*, ed: Mary Jo Binker
   (New York: Atria Books, 2018), 211.

6. Billy Graham quote, BrainyQuotes, https://www.brainyquote.com/quotes/
   billy_graham_394122.

7. "Go Forth into the World," A Collection of Prayers, https://acollectionof
   prayers.com/2016/08/01/go-forth-into-the-world/.

8. Winston Churchill quote, BrainyQuotes, https://www.brainyquote.com/
   quotes/winston_churchill_130619.

9. *Our Daily Bread,* June 4, 1997.

10. Deitrich Bonhoeffer, "Wedding Sermon from the Prison Cell," *Letters and
    Papers from Prison* (Philadelphia: Fortress Press, 2015), 82-87.

11. "1 Thessalonians 2:20," *Barnes' Notes on the Bible*, Bible Hub, https://bible hub.com/commentaries/1_thessalonians/2-20.htm#:~:text=%283%29%20 ministers%20of%20the%20gospel%20should%20be%20gentle%2C,a%20 mother%3B%201%20Thessalonians%202%3A7%2C%201%20 Thessalonians%202%3A11.

12. C.S. Lewis quotes, Goodreads, https://www.goodreads.com/ quotes/167976-at-present-we-are-on-the-outside-of-the-world.

13. Henry Van Dyke quote, Goodreads, https://www.goodreads .com/quotes/7572910-born-in-the-east-and-clothed-in-oriental -form-and#:~:text=%E2%80%9CBorn%20in%20the%20East%2C%20 and%20clothed%20in%20Oriental,land%20after%20land%20to%20 find%20its%20own%20everywhere.

14. Albert Smith quote, Bible Hub, quoting from The Biblical Illustrator, Electronic Database. Copyright © 2002, 2003, 2006, 2011 by BibleSoft, Inc. All rights reserved. Used by permission. BibleSoft.com.

15. "House Divided Speech," Abraham Lincoln, quoted from Neely, Mark E. Jr. 1982. *The Abraham Lincoln Encyclopedia*. New York: Da Capo Press, Inc., National Park Service, https://www.nps.gov/liho/learn/historyculture/ housedivided.htm.

16. "Lincoln, Grant, and the 1884 Election," National Park Service, https:// www.nps.gov/liho/learn/historyculture/lincolngrant.htm#:~:text=It%20 gave%20me%20a%20hearing%20on%20the%20great,cause%20of%20 liberty%20long%20after%20I%20am%20gone.%22.

17. Dorothy C. Haskin, *A Practical Guide to Prayer* (Chicago: Moody Press, 1951).

18. *The Collected Works of Jessie Penn-Lewis* (Jawbone Digital, 2012).

19. James Boswell, *The Life of Samuel Johnson* (New York: Penguin Classics, 1979).

20. Billy Graham, Answers, Billy Graham Evangelistic Association, November 8, 2021, https://billygraham.org/answer/ how-can-i-be-thankful-even-when-life-is-hard/.

To learn more about Harvest House books and
to read sample chapters, visit our website:

www.HarvestHousePublishers.com

HARVEST HOUSE PUBLISHERS
EUGENE, OREGON